Outdoor Entertaining

IDEA BOOK

NATALIE ERMANN RUSSELL

Outdoor Entertaining

IDEA BOOK

The Taunton Press

For my husband, Steve, my baby Sam, and my mom and dad, whose collective love and patience make everything possible.

Text © 2009 by Natalie Ermann Russell

Illustrations © 2009 by The Taunton Press, Inc.

The Taunton Press, Inc.,

63 South Main Street, PO Box 5506,

Newtown, CT 06470-5506

e-mail: tp@taunton.com

Editor: Erica Sanders-Foege

Copy editor: Karen Fraley

Jacket/Cover design: Alison Wilkes

Interior design: Kimberly Adis

Layout: Cathy Cassidy

Illustrator: Jean Tuttle

Cover photographers: Front cover (left, top to bottom): ©Jessie Walker Associates, Design: Pilar Simon; ©Mark Lohman, Design: Heather Lenkin of Lenkin Design; ©Jack Coyier Photography, Design: EPT Design; (middle): ©Jennifer Cheung and Steve Nilsson Photography, Design: Heather Lenkin of Lenkin Design; (right, top to bottom): ©Jack Coyier Photography, Design: Richard Krumwede, Architerra Design Group; ©Jack Coyier Photography, Design: Wendy Harper & Associates Landscape Architecture; © Tria Giovan Photography; Back cover: (top left) ©Chipper Hatter; (bottom left) ©Jack Coyier Photography; (bottom left) ©Jack Coyier Photography, Design: Ania Lejman Design Company; (bottom right) ©Jack Coyier Photography, Design: Richard Krumwede, Architerra Design Group

Library of Congress Cataloging-in-Publication Data

Russell, Natalie.

  Outdoor entertaining idea book / Natalie Ermann Russell.

     p. cm.

  ISBN 978-1-60085-061-5

  1. Entertaining. 2. Outdoor cookery. 3. Table setting and decoration. 4. Outdoor recreation. I. Title.

  GV1472.R87 2009

  793.2--dc22

                              2008032433

Printed in the United States of America

10 9 8 7 6 5 4 3 2 1

acknowledgments

any good host knows that entertaining is most successful (and fun) when it's a group effort. The same holds true for this book.

For their diligence and flexibility in capturing these beautifully landscaped homes, I'd like to thank all of the photographers and designers whose work is showcased on the following pages. A special thanks to photographers Jack Coyier, Mark Lohman, and Ken Gutmaker for their professionalism and eye for beauty. And to designers Heather Lenkin of Lenkin Design; Katie Moss of Katie Moss Landscape Design; Angie Coyier of Angie Coyier Landscape Architecture; and Pamela Palmer of ARTECHO Architecture and Landscape Architecture, thank you for sharing your knowledge and work, without which this book never would have happened. And, of course, a big note of gratitude for all of the homeowners who opened their homes to our cameras and shared a piece of their lives.

I'd also like to thank Taunton senior editor Erica Sanders-Foege, editorial assistant Catherine Levy, and photo editor Lucy Handley for all of their guidance and support; as well as all of the editors, the designers, and the production team who worked to make this book a reality. I promise to have you all over for an outdoor barbecue sometime soon.

—Natalie Ermann Russell

contents

introduction

as more and more Americans discover the boundless joys of outdoor living, they are inviting friends and family over to join in the fun.

Depending on what you like to do, where you live, and of course your budget, entertaining outdoors can take shape in a variety of ways. More often than not, it includes cooking and, of course, eating. The appliance of choice outdoors is the all-American grill, which in recent years has evolved from a wobbly three-legged cauldron into a fully appointed all-in-one kitchen.

Cooking goes hand in hand with dining, which also has advanced along with demand. Manufacturers are creating durable, weather-resistant tables, chairs, and cushions that make an outdoor dining area as well-appointed and comfortable as anything you'd find indoors.

The same holds true for an outdoor living room, which can include luxuries like fireplaces, fire pits, rugs, lamps, and sofas. Only instead of wallpaper or paint, it's surrounded by the natural scenery, be it a small garden, a mountain vista, or an ocean panorama.

Adding a feature like a pool or a garden room creates even more of a draw for friends and family. Pools, for example, scream fun for children and provide some much-needed relief from the summer heat for everyone else. They come in myriad shapes and sizes, and can be tailored to fit the parameters of your property. They are an invitation for your guests to be active as they enjoy living outdoors.

A garden room, on the other hand, is a blissfully peaceful destination. It often emphasizes relaxation and serves as a place where people can sit and visit with each other, the only distractions being the chirping of birds or rustling of squirrels.

Throughout this book, you'll discover just how many options there are when it comes to outdoor entertaining. As you explore, pull the ideas that appeal to you. Then synthesize them into a cohesive plan, and make your outdoor space uniquely—and enjoyably—yours.

cooking
outdoors

● ● ●

SOMEHOW PREPARING FOOD OUTDOORS NOT ONLY MAKES THE FOOD TASTE better, but it feels like less work. And being outside with the birds and the sunshine and the fresh air renders even the most tedious task pleasurable. That's the lure of the outdoor kitchen. If it's designed right, you can socialize and celebrate even as you prepare dinner.

The options with an outdoor kitchen run the gamut, from single portable grills to a kitchen setup with all of the bells and whistles: expansive countertops, a sink, cabinet storage, a refrigerator, a stovetop, and more. To figure out what you need, ask yourself how you intend to use the space and how many people you usually feed. What will you cook outdoors?

The answer almost always includes the word "grilled," but it can also include pizza (made in an outdoor brick oven) or Southern-style barbecue (prepared in a smoker). And it can include side dishes that need to be steamed, boiled, or sautéed, in which case you'll want a stovetop burner outside too.

A covered porch can be all you need to create the perfect outdoor kitchen. This one has protection from the elements and a sleek fireplace so the space can be used year-round. Because of the roof, however, a ventilation hood is required to redirect the smoke from the grill.

Of course, your budget will also play an important role in decision-making. But an outdoor kitchen doesn't have to break the bank; it really can be as basic or extravagant as you want.

Look for appliances, countertops, cabinetry, and other kitchen products designed to withstand the barrage of wind, rain, and sun. Many manufacturers are offering more and more durable products that need little if any maintenance. That's great because minimizing chores makes for easy living, and easy is what outdoor living is all about.

finding the perfect spot

●●● A GOOD OUTDOOR KITCHEN RESPONDS TO ITS SURROUNDINGS with functionality and beauty. It connects with the dining area and living area, so that it's as easy to socialize and converse as it is to set the table and serve the food. When the cook is at the grill, he will want to interact with the guests who are lounging on the couch. And he can ask for help without having to shout through walls and doors.

Instead of walls, rooms can be defined with half-walls (waist high), retaining walls, or plantings, or they can be elevated or lowered to elicit the feeling of discrete space. Shades, curtains, even awnings or umbrellas can also establish separate areas without blocking them off completely. And by strategically placing tables and islands, you can create desired "zones" of activity.

t he need for electricity, gas, and water hookups makes building a kitchen difficult for someone to do without the help of a pro. But there's no dearth of experts to help. A landscape architect or landscape designer in your area can be found listed on the American Society of Landscape Architects' website at www.asla.org; some outdoor appliance manufacturers offer design consultants you can work with to map out your dream outdoor kitchen; and many home improvement stores also often have help onsite.

When searching for a pro, approach it as you do any other time you need to hire someone to do a job for you. Meet with a handful of candidates to hear their ideas and peruse their portfolios. Ask for references so you can visit their completed projects and to hear unbiased opinions from past clients. And perhaps most important of all, choose someone with whom you feel comfortable. You don't want to be persuaded into purchasing features you don't like or can't afford.

TOP This clean-lined, modern grill unit includes built-in seating, so the diners can sit and watch as the chef is at work.

FACING PAGE A simple kitchen setup can provide all you'd want, even on a covered porch. A discreet refrigerator, grill, and sink get the job done so that the view of the yard can take center stage.

LEFT Keep a set of pots and pans in your outdoor kitchen, so that simple preparations can be taken care of onsite. While the grill heats, you can slice the peppers, put them on a baking sheet, and drizzle with oil. Then drop them onto the grill.

considering sight lines

● ● ● WHEN PLANNING AN OUTDOOR KITCHEN, you'll also want to keep views and focal points in mind. When you're in the space, what will you see? And to what will your eye be drawn? If you're the cook, an appealing view can make preparing a meal the best job of the evening. And a view can be everything from a colorful garden to an ocean vista to a fireplace across the patio. When you're thinking about where to put the appliances and grill, stand in the spot for a few minutes, turning in every direction to anticipate what your sight lines will be. Will your back be to your guests?

Next, stand where company might sit or stand and consider the views. Keep in mind how much privacy you would like, and how level the ground is (easier for installing the appliances). Answering these questions beforehand will keep you happy with the end result.

ABOVE
The fireplace is the focal point of this room, which gets its structure from the lighted pergola. With the grill located near the seating, no one has to go far to check on the steaks.

RIGHT
Connecting the kitchen and living area is a great way to ensure that guests are drawn to both. Here, the wood element in the countertop base ties in with the furniture in the living area.

LEFT Bringing a favorite holiday destination home is a great approach to designing an outdoor space because it will always feel like an escape. This setup was inspired by the homeowners' favorite vacation spot: Saint Tropez, in the south of France. The stucco wall and surrounding hedges provide a sense of privacy, also adding to the aura of "getaway."

More about...
KITCHEN LOCATION

When your outdoor kitchen is next to the house, hooking up the water, gas, and electricity for your appliances is much less expensive. Its proximity to the indoor kitchen can also make bringing food in and out easier and less time consuming. To improve efficiency even further, create a pass-through window between the indoor and outdoor kitchens, so you don't have to make multiple trips. And if the indoor kitchen opens onto the outdoor kitchen, you may consider using the same color palette and materials to keep it visually unified. This encourages your guests to wander freely between the two.

Having the kitchen adjacent to the house does have some downsides, though. The smoke from the grill can drift indoors. Choose a spot that is sheltered from the wind, so it won't be subject to smoke drift. Also keep the grill away from doors and windows. If this is difficult, you may need an over-grill hood, to ventilate the area.

A freestanding kitchen in the middle of the yard has its perks, especially if you have a large property. It will serve as a destination, drawing people outside and away from the house. Dinner outdoors in such a kitchen will feel like a retreat in your own backyard. And chances are, you'll have the space to keep a set of dishes, glassware, and flatware outside. Also, install a dishwasher or sink so you don't have to cart the dirty dishes inside.

workspaces in the outdoor kitchen

●●● WHEN PLOTTING YOUR OUTDOOR KITCHEN, approach it the same way you would any kitchen. The goal is to keep everything within reach but not cramped. Even a simple kitchen, with just a grill and a countertop, can be designed for maximum performance by making sure the equipment is out of the way of natural pathways to and from the house.

No matter how small your space, be sure to plan for at least some countertop. You will need it as a surface when you're chopping and preparing the food and even for serving. If the space does not lend itself to a fixed countertop, consider a work surface on wheels that can be moved to accommodate cooking as well as function as a small buffet.

LEFT Sometimes a high ceiling is essential for an outdoor kitchen. Here, the ceiling, generous counterspace, simple yet ample lighting, and a cooling ceiling fan all contribute to the space's success.

Asian Turkey Burger

by *Fine Cooking* staff

Yields 5 burgers

20 ounces ground turkey
  (either 99% or 97% lean)
2 tablespoons finely minced or grated fresh ginger
  (or more to taste)
2 tablespoons low-sodium soy sauce
2 tablespoons stone-ground mustard
Freshly ground pepper
5 honey wheat hamburger buns
Toppings: lettuce, sliced tomato,
  sliced red onion, wasabi mustard

Preheat grill to medium hot. In a large bowl, mix together the turkey, ginger, soy sauce, and mustard. Shape mixture into 5 four-ounce patties. Sprinkle pepper over top. Place on the grill for 6 minutes per side with the lid closed, or until completely done and no pink remains. Put one burger on each bun and top as desired.

FACING PAGE Even when it's raining, this Louisiana kitchen-dining area can be a wonderful retreat, thanks to the permanent roof. A few different seating options—at a full-size dining table or just a couple of chairs around a coffee table—give guests a choice and a chance to mingle.

RIGHT Symmetrical inset squares on either side of the grill add visual interest to the pattern of the concrete pavers, as does the grill that is set back from the front edge. Bar stools are ideal for movable seating, so that the cook can have companions (and helpers) as she works.

• setting up

When placing your appliances, start with the grill, the centerpiece of most kitchen setups. After you've accounted for at least 1½ feet of counterspace on each side, place the sink, refrigerator, and any other appliances you may be installing.

To connect the kitchen space with other outdoor living areas, namely the dining and living areas, you can use the same floor material, or unify it with a view or common plantings. Keeping all of the spaces unified allows people to roam freely among them and provides an open feeling that mimics that of nature.

ABOVE This compact cooking center has all the convenience of its indoor counterpart, including a ceiling overhead, and a full-size refrigerator. The brick, however, tells you it's outdoors. A ceiling fan and over-grill hood keep the fresh air circulating.

RIGHT This outdoor kitchen is as complete as the most elaborate indoor kitchen: plenty of storage, an island in the center, a wide range of appliances. The difference is the openness, which provides light and air.

Coffered ceilings add a surprising architectural element to an outdoor space. Here the view of the garden acts as a colorful backsplash for this stainless-steel-clad kitchen.

gallery

kitchen configurations

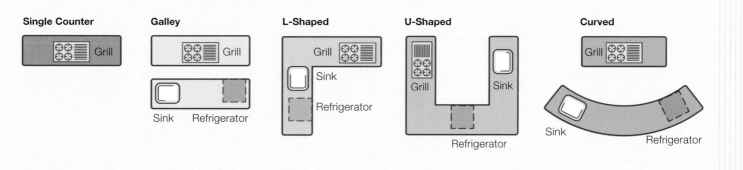

Single Counter

Galley

L-Shaped

U-Shaped

Curved

Grill

Grill

Grill

Sink

Refrigerator

Grill

Sink

Refrigerator

Grill

Sink

Refrigerator

Grill

Sink

Refrigerator

ABOVE This outdoor "kitchen" is simply a grill set amid a collection of terra cotta containers filled with herbs and lettuces. They add beauty and also provide the homeowner with delicious elements to work into the meal.

RIGHT Sometimes stone can make an outdoor cooking setup appear too massive, but here the light-colored Santa Barbara flagstone, used on the floor, backsplash and countertop base, is broken up by the gray grout to create a mosaic effect.

•a simple kitchen

As long as you have a cooking device, you've got yourself an outdoor kitchen. It doesn't have to be elaborate to get the job done. Even the most straightforward setup can provide workspace, storage space, lighting, and cooking surfaces. If it's on wheels, it can be transported around the yard or patio to take advantage of shady patches or to be close to the picnickers or diners wherever they may be. Or you can purchase a unit with a grill already fixed in a countertop island, so it looks like a more permanent kitchen.

There are almost endless style options for countertops, appliances, veneers, and storage. They can be stainless steel, wood, concrete, or stone; pared down or dressed up; contemporary or traditional. Grill-countertop combinations with artistic silhouettes are nearly works of art unto themselves. Some options even incorporate a bar area or hors d'oeuvre center, as if it were made specifically for the outdoor entertainer.

An enclosed porch is home to an outdoor kitchen with a grill, a ventilation hood, and plenty of countertop space. Sconces on the back wall provide enough light for nighttime cooking. And open shelving can be used for either display pieces or functional culinary tools.

Unused space next to stairs that lead up to an outdoor deck is the perfect spot for a grill—it's close enough that the host can still hear the conversation, but far enough away that the smoke won't waft into faces.

In this Southern California kitchen, the owners opted for a grill, stovetop, and mini refrigerator, but they left out a sink, since the nearby doors lead directly into the indoor kitchen. The stools tuck neatly under the far end of the countertop when not in use.

• keeping options open

If you're unsure about or can't afford a permanent kitchen at the moment, many manufacturers offer "components" that can be used either freestanding or fixed, (as in, dropped in or slid into a counter). That allows you the freedom to enjoy them separately, and then install them in a countertop layout as your budget allows over time. Doing so

can provide additional prep space and seating space for diners grazing on hors d'oeuvres or sitting at a bar/countertop.

It also opens up the option of adding other more elaborate appliances and storage features at a later date, when you're ready to take on the next phase of the project.

TOP This custom grill unit is made from stacked leger stone, which is continued on the backsplash. The countertop is granite, and extends about 18 inches on each side, the minimum recommended workspace width.

BOTTOM A grill set into a cement countertop unit is a contemporary touch and here works with the minimalist design of the home. An added goal was to avoid obstructing visibility for cook or guests, so the unit is open on the right side, with room for container plantings underneath.

r unning electricity, gas, and water outside can be expensive, but it will be worth it if you're planning to spend a good amount of time outdoors. If your budget is limited, you may want to take on the renovations in stages. But even so, you'd need to add these hookups while the ground is ripped up, at the beginning of the process. Not adding electricity, for example, can mean no amenities like blender drinks and no outdoor lamps, both of which can make entertaining outdoors so much more enjoyable.

Hooking up gas, electricity, and water is not an all-or-nothing proposition. There are ways to reduce costs and still get (almost) what you want. For example, instead of hooking up your outdoor kitchen to a gas line, you can install a propane-powered grill with a self-contained propane tank. The downside is that you will need to change out the propane tank and refill it when empty. Or you could opt for a charcoal grill, which doesn't need any hookup (but does require some maintenance on your part), or an electric grill, if you already plan to run electricity outside.

Even if you choose to have a sink outdoors, you may not need hot water, unless you install a dishwasher. The outdoor sink is best for rinsing hands, washing off fresh produce, and filling up a pot for cooking side dishes like corn on the cob or lobster. Cold water should suffice. But if you want the option of hot water, you could install an under-sink hot water heater so you don't have to pay to pump the hot water outside. Ask your contractor about the costs of the various options, and make a decision based on your personal needs.

a well-equipped kitchen

●●● FOR THE MORE ELABORATE KITCHEN, the options are as high-end as your budget allows. What makes you fall in love with an indoor kitchen are likely the same things that will make you swoon for your outdoor kitchen: Ample storage, convenient appliances, and a good layout are some of the main features to keep in mind. Then there are the additions that can turn your outdoor kitchen into a cook's paradise: built-in smoker, refrigerator, wine chiller, ice maker, wok cook-top, warming drawers, built-in trash can, lobster boiler, and the list goes on.

There's no one formula for a successful outdoor kitchen. Here, in lieu of a kitchen island, a farm table serves as a great area for prep or as a buffet. And a rocking chair is a convenient perch for those not involved in the meal preparation.

Stainless steel and brick is the palette for this outdoor kitchen, equipped with all of the essentials: a sink, refrigerator, grill, stovetop burners, and lots of storage. Choosing stainless appliances and fixtures nicely unifies the look and is practical—the material doesn't rust, keeps out water, and wears well.

all the bells and whistles

● ● ● AN OUTDOOR KITCHEN CAN BE WORKED into the corner to take advantage of unused space or it can stand out in the center of it all as the showpiece of the backyard. It can be one long counter or a user-friendly L shape with an island in the center. It can be close to chairs and couches so that the cook is always near the guests. Or it can be separated by a countertop or island so that the chef feels like the area is a clearly marked domain.

Before deciding on where you want your countertop-set grill, check with your local building codes; sometimes there are minimum distance requirements that this must be from the house. Also, consider sloping the countertop and floor to encourage rain runoff (and to prevent flooding). Consult with a pro about the best options for your site.

Placing the kitchen along one side of an outdoor living area organizes the space without making the appliances the focal point. Countertops at differing heights add interest and functionality.

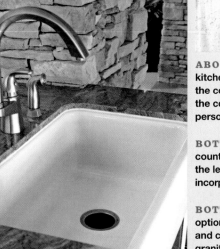

ABOVE Concrete, another great outdoor kitchen countertop material, can be poured so the countertop and sink are seamless. Here the concrete assumes a modern yet rustic personality.

BOTTOM LEFT Stained into the concrete countertops is the homeowners' monogram—the letter B. The concrete backsplash tiles also incorporate the Victorian character of the home.

BOTTOM RIGHT Granite, one of the best options for outdoor countertops, is durable and cleans up easily. Here rainbow-hued granite brings a splash of color to this outdoor kitchen, especially when the sunshine hits it just so.

COUNTERTOP BASICS

inside or outside, countertops must be durable. But being outside requires an extra dose of sturdiness, since it needs to withstand wind, rain, sun, and any other weather that comes your way. It also should be able to tolerate high heat, since it will be next to a hot, flaming grill. In other words, you don't want to have a plywood countertop topped with tile or laminate; the wood is too flammable.

Some of the best materials are stainless steel, brick, stone, stucco, and concrete. However, many of those materials (all but stainless) have to be sealed and resealed every few years to prevent staining and bacteria growth.

When it comes to cleanup, the ideal countertop is simply hosed down. For example, if the countertop, walls, and floor are made of concrete, you can hose down the whole place (as long

as the cabinets are closed and are water-tight).

If your countertop is exposed to the sun, choose a material that doesn't absorb heat. This means you want to opt for light-colored materials over dark-colored. Also look for materials that are scratch resistant and UV stable, so the color won't fade.

grills

● ● ● WHAT INSPIRES PEOPLE TO INSTALL AN OUTDOOR KITCHEN is often the lure of the grill. It imparts a special flavor in foods of all kinds—from vegetables and meats to fruits and even desserts. The selection of grills on the market these days allows you to find one that meets your practical needs, as well as your aesthetic taste.

There are hybrid grills that give you the option of charcoal, wood, and/or gas on any given day, and there are models powered by electricity. There are easy-to-light gas options and ones with customized grates for creating sear marks. The prices run the gamut too: on the low end, you can find a simple model for $100; on the high end, you can spend thousands of dollars.

Cooker with a ceramic interior for faster cooking.

Pizza Dough for the Grill

by Frank McClelland

**Figure one to two balls of dough per person.
Make two separate batches if you need more dough.
Yields dough for 8 small pizzas**

1 package (2¼ teaspoons.) active dry yeast
   or 1 ounces fresh yeast
1¼ cups warm water (about 105°F)
4¼ cups all-purpose flour
2 teaspoons kosher salt
1¼ cups olive oil; more for the bowl

❶ Stir the yeast into the water; let sit for 15 minutes. Combine the flour and salt in the bowl of a stand mixer fitted with the dough hook or in a large bowl. On low speed in the stand mixer or stirring with a wooden spoon, slowly add the yeast mixture and the olive oil alternately to the flour. Knead for 6 minutes on low speed in the stand mixer or on a floured surface by hand until it becomes elastic. The dough should feel soft and just a little sticky. If it feels grainy or dry, add 1 tablespoon warm water at a time (up to 1¼ cup). Knead for another 2 minutes by hand on a floured surface.

❷ Transfer the dough to a lightly oiled bowl that's at least twice the size of the dough and cover with a damp dishtowel. Let rise at room temperature until almost doubled, about 1 hour. The dough is ready when you poke a finger in it and it holds the impression.

❸ Punch down the dough and divide it into 8 balls. Put each ball on a floured surface and, with your hands, flatten and stretch it into a disk that's about ½ inch thick. The dough will be fairly elastic and will tend to spring back. Cover each piece with plastic and let rest for 5 minutes. Stretch or roll each disk into an 8- to 10-inch round about ⅛ inch thick (the thinner, the better). Line a rimmed baking sheet with parchment or waxed paper and layer the rounds on it with a sheet of parchment or waxed paper between each. Use the dough immediately or cover and refrigerate for up to 4 hours.

Adapted from *Fine Cooking* 66, p.38

TOP Gas grill with cutting board, push-button start, and a slide-out propane tank tray.

BOTTOM Liquid propane hybrid grill; cooks with charcoal, wood, and gas using interchangeable grilling drawers.

More about...
GAS VS. CHARCOAL

ⓘ t's a personal preference, but there are plusses and minuses to gas and charcoal. Gas grills are easier to clean, easier to light, and produce arguably more healthful food (recent studies have linked char-grilled foods with certain cancers). Gas grills are also more eco-friendly, as they emit about half as much greenhouse gas as charcoal does. Gas grills are also the most popular choice (9 out of 10 buyers opt for one).

On the other hand, some say charcoal grills offer better flavor. But charcoal grills can require more maintenance and emit more volatile organic compounds (VOCs), which have been linked with a variety of health problems. If you opt for charcoal, there are ways to be more eco-friendly: use sustainably harvested wood chips or all-natural briquettes, which are less damaging to the environment.

If you simply can't decide, the solution may lie in a hybrid. These are often hooked up to a gas source, but have drawers for wood and coal, to impart the flavor. Simply put, it's the best of both worlds.

TOP A movable grill cart with stovetop burners and an oven.

MIDDLE Stainless-steel gas grill, inspired by Japanese yakitori carts.

BOTTOM Stainless-steel gas grill with teak accents, slate countertops, and option for infrared burners. The drawer hides the propane tank; it can be hooked up to a gas line instead.

grills: form and function

The look of the grill is arguably second to the food it's able to produce, but as the most essential outdoor kitchen appliance, it's important nonetheless. Grill manufacturers are taking this into account by making models styled with a modern flair or even a sculptural silhouette.

No detail is too small. Even the grate itself can be customized with particular shapes or monograms. That said, utility is paramount, and the design reflects that. There are hooks for grill tools, drawers for condiments, and built-in burners for side dishes or sauces. These features along with ease of use and maintenance should be considered. Look into the costs for replacement parts for the brand you select, because even many of the high-end models require repairs, and some parts can be expensive and hard to find.

ABOVE Charcoal grill and smoker, made of weather-proof ceramic.

LEFT This stainless-steel gas grill with a sculptural shape, can be left out to look like a piece of artwork in the garden.

choosing small appliances

●●● ALMOST ANY KITCHEN APPLIANCE OR DEVICE YOU CAN IMAGINE can be tailored for outside. You can have anything from a keg tap to a pizza oven to a smoker. Look for Energy Star rated appliances, which use gas and/or electricity more efficiently and will reduce your utility bills.

Also look for "UL" certification, which indicates a certain level of safety (UL stands for United Laboratories, an independent safety tester). Also for safety, you want appliances that can be plugged into GFCI (ground-fault circuit interrupter) outlets. Know the surroundings in which you're putting them. If it's something with a protruding chimney, like a wood-fired pizza oven, look up to make sure you're clear of power lines, and be sure it isn't placed right below a tree (a fire hazard).

If you live in a region that has cold winters, or winters at all, you may opt for appliances that have been winterized, so you can use the space year-round. Wood-fired pizza is just as wonderful in colder months as it is in the summer.

Refrigerated drawer for beverages.

appliances

1

2

3

4

5

6

7

8

1 Outdoor refrigerated beer keg tapper.

2 Separate cooktop unit.

3 Beverage cooler with a built-in bottle-cap opener.

4 Wood-fired pizza oven.

5 Dishwasher drawer for smaller loads.

6 Smoker box.

7 Ventilation hood for covered kitchens.

8 Pizza oven.

finishing touches

●●● WITH THE BIG ELEMENTS OF THE KITCHEN IN PLACE, you can now move on to the details that give it the character you're looking for. Think about what you like style-wise on the inside of the house, and use that as a starting point for the outside. It's nice to tie the two together with similar floor materials and lighting fixtures, so there is a consistency as you move from one to the other. It's also important to take the house's architecture into consideration, so they harmoniously complement each other and make for a seamless transition.

BELOW
Convenience is the key to cooking outdoors. Rely on foods that are in season for incomparable flavor and nutritional value.

FACING PAGE TOP LEFT The right lighting can enhance the style of your outdoor kitchen in subtle ways. This lantern-style fixture brings old world charm to a new home.

FACING PAGE BOTTOM LEFT Determining if a piece of meat is rare, medium rare, or well done is much easier when you can actually see it. A small light fixed to the grill provides sufficient task lighting directly where it's needed.

FACING PAGE BOTTOM RIGHT So that bulky light fixtures don't disrupt the look of this kitchen, the designer hid them within the structure of the pergola. They are aimed at the stovetop, grill, and other appliances, without overlighting the adjacent dining area.

● lighting

As is true of inside, outdoor kitchens need task lighting so you can see as you chop, sauté, and prepare meals. During the summer it may not be as much of a problem, when the days are long and the natural sunlight lingers into the evening. But come fall, it can get dark well before dinnertime. To provide the needed light, there are many options. You can attach a clip-on light to the grill itself, or you can use a freestanding outdoor lamp. There are grills that become illuminated when the lid is opened, much like a refrigerator. That means you don't have to carry a flashlight with you every time you go to check on the steaks.

If you have an overhang, ceiling, or nearby wall, then your options are even more varied. Ceiling fixtures can be hung from above, and sconces can illuminate the wall and the workspace.

keeping kitchen appliances protected from rain, wind, and sun can be helpful but isn't necessary. Some people prefer to cook in the wide open, feeling like they're truly out surrounded by nature. Others prefer the comfort and security of an overhang so that they can cook even when it's raining. Still others like a combination of the two, and find a solution by installing umbrellas, awnings, or other retractable weatherproof coverings.

If you plan to have an overhang over the cooking area, be sure to choose a nonflammable material. Or install an overhead ventilated hood made specifically for outdoors to properly redirect the smoke from the grill.

storage

●●● ARE YOU CLOSE ENOUGH TO THE INDOOR KITCHEN that you can quickly hop inside to fetch an extra plate or platter? If the answer is no, you may consider keeping a separate set of dishes and beverages outside so there's no trekking back and forth. Look for cabinets that are weather tight so the moisture and dust can't get inside. Many outdoor cabinets are made of rugged stainless steel or high-density polyethylene (HDPE, which is so durable that it's used on boat decks) because they are extremely hard-wearing. If you live in a dry climate, you might opt for wood, but make sure it's a type that will withstand moisture, such as cedar or teak.

Since space is almost always at a premium, storage in your kitchen area should be maximized. Cabinets with pocket doors, which slide from side to side, will leave pathways clear even when open. Built-in benches with a hinged lid along a wall can double as storage for kitchen-seating cushions. And refrigerated drawers provide additional storage for things like juice boxes, one of life's necessities if there are young children in your house.

BELOW
Translucent cabinets make the dishes and glassware part of the décor, allowing their colors to shine through. It's a more modern approach to cabinetry, but keeps the dishes protected from pollen, dust, and everything else that comes with outdoor cooking.

FACING PAGE TOP LEFT This stovetop unit comes with storage space underneath, great for silverware and napkins that might be used for outdoor dining, or for wooden spoons and other necessities for stirring the contents of a pot on the burner.

FACING PAGE TOP RIGHT For kitchens without built-in cabinets, freestanding units are ideal. This stainless-steel tool cart on wheels is used to hold grilling utensils. It also brings more countertop prep space to the equation, and provides a good surface for a heat lamp.

ike counter materials, floors should be able to withstand weather extremes. An added consideration, however, is safety. If it rains or someone spills a drink, you don't want it to become slippery. Even if you have an overhang or some other covering for partial or complete protection from the elements, it's better to choose a stone material, brick, or concrete that will not become slick. Glazed tiles and even some materials that aren't shiny can be dangerous when wet.

Think about maintenance too when you're choosing a floor material. An outdoor space shouldn't require scrubbing on your hands and knees, so pick one that can be hosed down and that will look good with the patina of age.

Most floor materials conducive to the outdoor kitchen will also work in the living and dining areas. In the kitchen, though, it's very important that the floor is level so the appliances will work properly.

LEFT Drawers and cabinets here hold all that's needed for outdoor cooking. One of the most popular materials is stainless steel because of its durability. This kitchen uses both painted wood and stainless for storage, marrying old and new styles quite successfully.

outdoor dining

● ● ●

EATING OUTSIDE IS A LIFESTYLE, AN EXTENSION OF INDOOR LIVING, but with nature as the wallpaper. It is the obvious companion to grilling outside, which is the driving force behind much of the outdoor activity in the United States. But outdoor dining rooms can be used even when the grill isn't turned on. They can play host to everything from a takeout-pizza party to a three-course sit-down meal. And they can be any size, any extravagance.

Figuring out what you need depends on how you plan to use the space. If you and your guests have children, for example, creating a little dining area especially for them will keep the fidgeting at bay. Or if you tend to host numerous cocktail parties, you'll want several conversation spots where people can gather to eat and schmooze.

If you plan to entertain frequently with large dinner parties, you'll want a large table. And a few smaller tables scattered around the property allow you to accommodate extra guests that may show up unannounced. Or you might opt for a combination of only smaller rectangular and square tables. For a more formal dinner, they can be lined up to create one long table; and for a more casual, intimate gathering, you can use one to serve off of and one for eating.

No matter what you choose, creating an outdoor dining area is an opportunity to design a space around your lifestyle, rather than the other way around.

Dining outdoors has a way of lifting everyone's spirits. This teak and aluminum table-and-chairs set has a decidedly dynamic, modern tone. It's casual enough for daytime and easily transformed for a more formal occasion at night.

where to put the table

FOR YOUR DINING TABLE, there are many factors to consider. Proximity to the house is important, so that the host has an easy path back inside to fetch the bottle of salad dressing or ketchup that she may have forgotten.

Also keep in mind how you use the space around the area: For example, if your party gets carried away having a good time, you'll want to make sure that they are far enough away from the house so to not wake up sleeping kids. It's a good idea to tailor the placement of the outdoor spaces to fit your particular situation.

Also consider the views from the table. These could be of the pool or the house, or of an ocean, mountains, or a vista in the distance. A shady spot is also ideal for dining, since lunch is always more enjoyable when the sun isn't blazing down and wilting your food. To figure out where you want the dining area, set a chair in a few different spots, and sit there at different times of the day to find the setting that simply feels best.

BELOW
Poolside dining is almost always magical. At night, the lights reflect off of the water. Comfortable armchairs enhance the experience. A beautiful brick wall adds privacy.

placing the table

Minimum Clearance for Dining Table

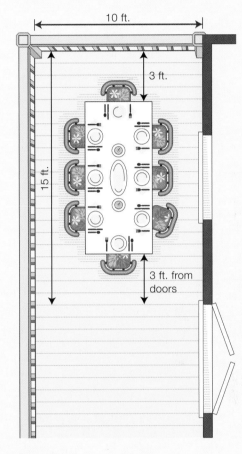

10 ft.

3 ft.

15 ft.

3 ft. from doors

Bistro Table

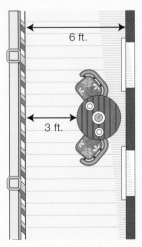

6 ft.

3 ft.

TOP Decorating a covered patio can really transform it. Here, faux curtains (they can't be drawn) with black piping add an elegant finish. A lightweight dining table with chairs is easy to pull out from under the overhang when the weather is agreeable.

BOTTOM A bistro table and chairs is placed just beside a water fountain, which provides a relaxing gurgle as you dine.

choosing a furniture style

● ● ● MARRYING YOUR BACKYARD LANDSCAPE WITH THE RIGHT STYLE of table and chairs is as much about beauty as it is about brawn. Gone are the days when the only options are either ornate and over-the-top or bland and boring. Today there is chunky teak, contemporary plexi, and durable aluminum. There are styles for the cottage lover, the modernist, the fan of arts and crafts, the minimalist, and almost any other style you could want. There are new products available at big box stores or specialty designers, or there are antiques and vintage items that can set a retro mood.

To figure out what style you want, look inside your home: Carrying the aesthetic of the inside to the outdoor spaces creates cohesion and ties everything together. And of course sit in the chairs pulled up to the table to test out comfort, height, and sturdiness.

BELOW
Sometimes all you need is a patio and a place to sit. Clean and modern, a white plastic table and chairs are complemented nicely by lime green melamine dishes. The oval table shape fits well in this dining area that's bounded by a wall of ivy.

ABOVE A happy mix of traditional and modern styles is achieved with this banquette dining area. The neutral cushions never fall out of fashion as long as throw pillows are changed out as tastes change.

RIGHT It's not hard to create the feel of a flowery English garden. In this room, a painted-wood dining table with distressed edges pairs nicely with the painted metal chairs and the rectangular mirror on the buffet. Finally, the painted ceiling brings it all together

More about...
FURNITURE MATERIALS

What your furniture is made of plays a big role in its style. Aluminum and plastic are often contemporary, for example; wicker and teak, more traditional. Beyond style, you'll want to consider how easy it is to care for your furniture. Teak, for example, needs to be oiled, and weathers from a warm honey color to a stormy gray.

Aluminum and plastic are easy to care for and can be hosed down or wiped clean with just soap and water. Antique wicker requires a bit more care. Hosing it down could incur damage; instead, wipe with a damp cloth and store it during the harsh winter months.

Another factor to consider is rust. Aluminum won't rust, but other metals like steel and wrought iron can when the paint chips (especially if a furniture cover traps the moisture inside). Look for powder-coated pieces, which have proven to be more durable than those that are covered with regular paint. Also consider the cushions. Can the covers be removed and thrown into the washing machine? Or must you spot clean them with a damp cloth? Your maintenance routine should affect your choice as much as looks do.

TOP A wrought-iron table and chairs say "traditional" in this otherwise rustic outdoor space that also features cobblestones and a mortarless stone wall.

family meals

●●● THE TABLE FOR A FAMILY GATHERING is a very personal situation. What you choose and how you set it up depends on the number of people you're feeding, first and foremost. If you need flexibility to accommodate a large group or several children, a bench is a great solution because you can squeeze several into the space (if you had chairs, each would take up an equal amount of room, no matter if it's occupied by an adult or child). And you may consider a table with leaves or fold-down sides so you can expand when friends come over too.

Another issue to consider is the type of cuisine you usually prepare. If it's casual and rarely involves a main course, but rather hors d'oeuvres and snacks, then you may consider counter-height tables so people can graze as they mingle, or lower coffee tables so people can gather around for snacking and chatting.

ABOVE Family dining almost always requires passing platters of food, so an umbrella extending from the middle of the table can eat up precious space. Here, the perfect solution is a cantilevered umbrella whose base is camouflaged by a cluster of container plantings.

FACING PAGE LEFT In this casual country dining area, a built-in bench accommodates the family and then some. The seating arrangement is a favorite with the kids of the house, who enjoy having a special place to sit together.

TOP Casual dining can be quite beautiful, even with just the basics. Folding chairs add a splash of color to this corner of the yard. And everything is portable enough that when it rains, it can all be dragged into the garage without much fuss.

BOTTOM With several dining spots around the patio, this Sonoma home takes advantage of the great California weather and is ideal for parties big or small. The open layout and sliding glass walls encourage guests to move easily from inside to out.

dinner is served

●●● THE SETUP YOU CHOOSE SHOULD ALSO FACILITATE CONVERSATION and allow for passing of food with ease. Round tables can encourage dialogue, since everyone, no matter where they're sitting, can make eye contact. On the other hand, square and rectangular tables can simplify passing dishes, since it's usually easier to reach across. The shape of the table will also be dictated, however, by the dimensions and setup of your space.

At least one or two people (i.e., the hosts) should be in a position where they can excuse themselves easily to fetch drinks or side dishes from the kitchen. Or if you have children, you'll want to design the seating so everyone can easily get up from the table without having to ask others to move out of the way.

This awning-covered dining area has an air of formality, no matter what's on the menu. A view of the pool below makes this a lovely place for brunch, with perhaps a dip afterward. When there's a need for more privacy or to block out the sun, the weather-resistant-fabric curtains can be drawn.

LEFT This wooden pergola establishes the dining area and allows for an electrified lantern to be suspended from one of the beams. The high walls and double-door gate give this space the feeling of a hidden paradise.

ABOVE Having a kids' table needn't be just for special occasions. It's a great idea even when just a couple of neighbors drop by for grilled burgers. The adults can keep an eye out while the children feel somewhat independent. Other times, it can be used as a buffet spot.

RIGHT A nook of a dining area utilizes the limited square footage efficiently. A teak bench with pillows is pushed against the house to create a cozy feeling. Container plantings and trees add to the intimate setting.

LEFT With a view like this, who wants walls? A gas fireplace and lanterns add just the right light, while the romantic wrought iron arches stand out like artwork against the sky. Candlelight on the table further sets the mood.

FACING PAGE TOP LEFT This festive setup is casual enough for family meals too. Using the same colors on the table that appear in the garden ties everything together. Green dishware mimics the plantings. A roaring fire and candle chandelier add comfort and beauty.

FACING PAGE TOP RIGHT A sunroom gives the homeowners flexibility when it comes to entertaining. Glass walls allow for unobstructed views of the garden outside, while potted topiaries bring a little of the outdoors in.

•dining with guests

If you entertain frequently outdoors and like to invite over neighbors and colleagues for food a notch above what you'd serve the family, there are many ways to set the mood for such a special occasion. There's the food, of course, which even on the grill can take on an elegant vibe. Grilled fish, meats, and chicken taste wonderful, and really make a plate look beautiful with lovely grill marks. The simplicity of grilled foods, from appetizer to dessert, makes a strong statement without much fuss: grilled whole fish stuffed with fresh herbs from the garden, grilled tomatoes and peppers that can be diced into a smoky salsa, even grilled peaches served with a cool scoop of ice cream.

Farmer's Market Quesadillas

by *Fine Cooking* staff

Yields 4 quesadillas

5 tablespoons vegetable oil
1 cup small-diced fresh, mild chiles,
   such as Anaheim or poblano
   (from about 2 large chiles)
1½ cups small-diced summer squash
   (from about 2 small zucchini, yellow
   squash, or yellow crookneck)
Kosher salt and freshly ground
   black pepper
1 cup fresh corn kernels
   (from 2 medium ears)
⅛ teaspoons chipotle chile powder
1 cup diced tomato
   (from 2 small tomatoes)
¼ cup chopped fresh cilantro
1 tablespoons fresh lime juice
Four 9-inch flour tortillas
2 cups grated sharp cheddar (8 ounces)
Sour cream for serving (optional)

❶ Heat the oven to 200°F. Fit a cooling rack over a baking sheet and put in the oven.

❷ Heat 1 tablespoon of the oil in a 12-inch skillet over medium-high heat until hot. Add the chiles and cook, stirring, until soft, 3 to 4 minutes. Add the squash, season with salt and pepper, and cook, stirring, until the squash softens and starts to brown, 3 to 4 minutes. Stir in the corn and chipotle powder and cook 2 minutes more. Spoon into a bowl, let cool for a few minutes, and then fold in the tomato, cilantro, and lime juice. Season to taste with salt and pepper. Set aside ¾ cup of the mixture.

❸ Lay several layers of paper towel on a work surface. Wipe out the skillet, put it over medium-high heat, and add 1 tablespoon of the oil. When it's hot, put one tortilla in the pan. Quickly distribute ½ cup of the cheese evenly over the tortilla and about a quarter of the remaining vegetable mixture over half the

tortilla. When the underside of the tortilla is browned, use tongs to fold the cheese-only side over the vegetable side. Lay the quesadilla on the paper towels, blot for a few seconds, and then move it to the rack in the oven to keep warm while you repeat with the remaining oil and tortillas. Cut the quesadillas into wedges and serve immediately with the reserved vegetable mixture and sour cream.

From *Fine Cooking* 87, pp. 78A

dressing up for company

●●● THE TABLE DECOR IS ANOTHER WAY TO MAKE A DINNER MORE FORMAL. A tablecloth thrown over even a picnic table can elevate the space to dinner-party caliber. Glass goblets and cloth napkins can also lend the air of a special occasion. Lighting sets the mood as well, through intensity and the style of each fixture.

The style of décor itself can tell visitors that this will be a special experience. If you do a lot of formal entertaining, you may opt for styles that can be easily dressed up. If you host one or two parties a year but also eat outside with the family, a more flexible setup that can go either formal or informal is a more practical choice.

RIGHT For a cocktail party, covering an inexpensive metal or wood round table in a plain cloth can dress it up nicely.

FACING PAGE TOP A plain-colored tablecloth can be transformed with a vibrant runner laid overtop. Even the flower is part of the palette of this dinner party.

FACING PAGE BOTTOM A simple metal structure embodies romantic elegance, thanks to the oversize seersucker tablecloth and the crystal chandelier.

Grilled Swordfish with Lemon, Dill and Cucumber Sauce

by *Fine Cooking* staff

Yields 6 servings

FOR THE SAUCE:
1 medium English cucumber,
   peeled and finely diced to yield 2 cups
2 tablespoons fresh lemon juice
½ teaspoons granulated sugar
Kosher salt and freshly ground black pepper
¼ cup extra-virgin olive oil
2 tablespoons minced fresh dill
1 tablespoons minced shallot
2 teaspoons minced fresh mint

FOR THE SWORDFISH:
1½ tablespoons olive oil; more for brushing the grill
Six 1¼-inch-thick swordfish steaks (6 to 8 ounces each)
1 teaspoon kosher salt

❶ Put the cucumber in a medium bowl. Add the lemon juice and the sugar, toss to combine, and season with salt and pepper to taste. Stir in the olive oil, dill, shallot, and mint, and add more salt and pepper if necessary. Let sit for 30 minutes to allow the flavors to marry. Taste for seasoning again just before serving and adjust if necessary.

❷ Clean and oil the grates on a gas grill and heat the grill to medium high, or prepare a medium-hot charcoal fire.

❸ Meanwhile, generously coat both sides of the swordfish with the oil and season both sides with salt. Let the fish sit at room temperature for 15 minutes (while the grill heats). Grill the swordfish steaks directly over the heat source (covered on a gas grill, uncovered on a charcoal grill), without touching, until they have good grill marks, 2 to 4 minutes. Flip the steaks and grill until the second sides have good grill marks and the fish is done to your liking, another 2 to 4 minutes. (Check for doneness by slicing into one of the thicker pieces.) Serve immediately, topped with the cucumber sauce.

From *Fine Cooking 86*, pp. 42

entertaining large groups

●●● IF YOUR OUTDOOR ENTERTAINING IS ALWAYS A BIG PRODUCTION, perhaps with hired help to prepare and serve the food, this will affect how you design and lay out your space. Say you have an annual party for officemates or employees, and a caterer does all of the work. The dining area should be easy to access for the servers, but not so close that the behind-the-scenes chaos in the kitchen or prep area is visible to the guests.

You also may consider setting aside a courtyard or other open space so that you can bring in rented tables for the parties. The choices you make in the kitchen should also reflect this lifestyle: warming drawers to help keep the main course toasty as the hors d'oeuvres are passed; a refrigerator for keeping ingredients like whipped cream and cheeses chilled until they're served; and extra storage for serving trays and platters.

46

FACING PAGE For these homeowners, entertaining is one of the main reasons for having a finished outdoor space. Because they like to host large parties, the pool deck has room for several tables. There's even additional seating on the built-in concrete bench that wraps around the tree.

ABOVE This farm table, with its mix-and-match seating and eclectic bouquet, conveys a casual style, while the wine goblets and cloth napkins convey it's a special day. A candle chandelier and blown-glass balls hanging from the branches above join the celebration.

More about...
PARTY RENTALS

for big celebrations, or even just for larger-than-normal dinner parties, renting can be a cost-effective and convenient option. Especially if you're cooking all of the food yourself, you may want to hire a rental company to come in and set up the tables, chairs, tablecloths, glasses, and place settings. Then when you're done, they take it all away, as is, no washing necessary—a real treat after your hosting duties are complete. If the gathering is large enough, you may also consider renting a tent or overhang.

Or you could choose to rent just one or two of those items. Renting glassware, for example, is relatively inexpensive and adds an air of formality without the worry of breakage. If you need only a couple of extra tables, many retail stores sell party tables and chairs that fold up and that can even be put away in a bag, so you'll have them again for next time. The options are much more attractive than the wobbly card tables of yesteryear.

tables
for two

●●● THE BEST PART ABOUT DINING WITH JUST ONE OTHER PERSON is the intimacy of the moment. That feeling can be carried through to the layout of the spot itself. Oftentimes a secluded nook, surrounded by greenery, can make you and your dining companion feel like the only two people in the world. A table for two also can make use of otherwise wasted space: crannies or corners that are too small for other furnishings can make for a great mini dining room. Tables can be round or square; chairs can be elaborate or basic—and all will work very nicely in an intimate space.

Where you place your setup should reflect the lifestyle you lead. If, for instance, you sit at the table to read the paper with your coffee every morning, think about taking advantage of any sunrise view. Or if you frequent it for an après-work cocktail and some conversation about your day, keep the sunset in mind.

LEFT A couple of metal folding chairs and a bistro table make for an idyllic setting to sit and admire the gardening handiwork. The flagstone porch entry with its menagerie of container plantings is just the beginning; beyond the iron arch are more gardens.

FACING PAGE LEFT In a gem of a spot, a hidden courtyard is home to a small dining table brightened up with a lively tablecloth and cushions. The sunset colors are in keeping with the Moroccan-style gateway, creating an exotic dining experience at home.

TOP Lighting can set the mood, especially with a table for two. Here, a gas-powered French Colonial–style lamp is the source.

BOTTOM A table for two needn't always be small. Any table will suffice when the settings are next to each other, which, in this case, allows both diners to share the view. The floral centerpiece is set between the place settings, instead of in the exact middle, to make this larger table feel more intimate.

bars

● ● ● IF ENTERTAINING AT YOUR HOUSE INCLUDES COCKTAIL HOUR, an outdoor bar is a decadent way to indulge the grown-ups. A bar can be a freestanding unit on wheels, or part of the kitchen counter setup alongside the grill. It can have a sink, for rinsing and for making drinks, or it can be just an extension of the countertop with a few bar stools, for which you'd need just a few extra feet. In fact, putting a bar at one end of the kitchen countertop is a great use of space, since many barstools can be pushed under the counter itself and take up no additional square footage.

Prefabricated versions cost a couple grand (not including stools), but high-end ones can run five times that. You might opt instead to have one designed to fit your custom kitchen, and spend as little or as much as the budget allows. Popular features include built-in ice chests and trashcans, cupboards and shelves for storage, cutting boards for prep, and wine chillers. Consider what you typically serve from the bar to make your decision: If you're a fan of frozen drinks, you'll want an outlet for plugging in a blender; if you only do beer, consider including a beer tap.

BELOW
This bar unit is outfitted with all of the necessities: a refrigerator, an ice chest, a sink, a towel rack, and a stereo system.

More about...
BAR AND SEATING MEASUREMENTS

there is actually a science to installing a bar area tailored to your needs. It used to be that the standard bar height was between 40 and 42 inches, but today more people are opting for a raised bar height (44 to 48 inches) so that guests can dine while they stand, as in a party setting. With the standard height, you'd need chairs that are between 28 and 30 inches high; for the raised bar, 34 to 36 inches.

The widths of the seats also matter, since this measurement affects how many people you can fit along any given space. For example, for seats 16 to 18 inches wide, you would need to budget for at least 22 inches for each; between 19 and 22 inches, budget for at least 25 inches. And keep in mind that if the barstools swivel or if they have arms, you will need a few inches more for each.

ABOVE Putting a bar area in the same space as the dining table isn't just for restaurants. Here, lantern-style lights and the dark wood corbels set against the light bar add a European flair.

LEFT This outdoor bar isn't completely outdoors. While the barstools reside in the sunshine, the service and storage stay inside. The windows crank out to connect the two.

ABOVE This Celtic wall bar area doubles as countertop space for the grillmaster. The undulating concrete counter is indented for each of the chairs.

setting the table

●●● HOW YOU SET YOUR TABLE IS A REFLECTION OF YOUR MOOD and the mood of the event. It's like a wardrobe for your outdoor dining area, so you should approach it as such: sweat pants for lounging, and cocktail dress for a soiree.

Use your linens, dishes, glassware, and silverware to make a fashion statement. You can go with eclectic or contemporary, traditional or international. But you also want to tie in the festive, organic atmosphere of the outdoors, even if you tend toward the formal. And because you're outside, look for durable materials that are hard to break and won't fade in the sun.

ABOVE Tables need not be fancy to look welcoming. Boldly striped napkins with a red tablecloth and simple earthenware ensure a happy meal.

LEFT A Virginia covered porch is home to this well-appointed table. The fruits de mer centerpiece of shells, coral, and starfish hint at the meal to come. The sideboard makes it as complete of a dining room as any you'd find indoors.

ABOVE Against a black table, black and white place settings are quite sharp. These contemporary plates, napkins, and placemats are softened with a bouquet of fragrant lilac. On a slatted table, placemats dress up the whole setup.

LEFT A beautiful wood farm table and simple cloth napkins and glasses don't outshine the main event—the food— but set a warm and welcoming scene.

More about...
TABLECLOTHS

When searching for a tablecloth for outdoor use, you want to keep a few things in mind. First, it should be easy to clean—preferably something you can just throw in the washer. If it is dry-clean only, it's going to need to be cleaned every time you use it, because outdoor entertaining is almost always a messy ordeal (creatures, flowers, and food all contribute).

A tablecloth should also be made of a material that will be durable, and heavy enough that a gust of wind won't lift it off. Appropriate tablecloth materials include oilcloth, which has a plasticized coating and can be wiped down with a wet sponge; canvas, which is the material of choice for boat sails, and therefore you can be sure is durable, wears well, and is almost always machine washable; polyester, which repels moisture because it's a type of plastic; and vinyl, which is also made of plastic and can be wiped down easily while still on the table. Of course, be sure to take measurements of your table before going to the store.

The color of the sky is brought into this table through the striped damask tablecloth. In keeping with the natural theme, whole fruit makes a vivid centerpiece when arranged with a few leaves on cake stands.

This aluminum table has decorative ceramic tile on top so that there's little dressing up to be done. To keep napkins from blowing away in the breeze, they're tucked under the plates. And little potted plants serve as place cards.

Red is the favorite color of this homeowner, so she brings it into almost everything, even the salt and pepper grinders. The cheery pattern carries from the chair cushions to the placemats to the plates. These plates are actually melamine, and the glasses plastic.

• linens

Even outside, tablecloths, placemats, and cloth napkins are appropriate. And they needn't be formal: The colors and patterns available today can set a jaunty mood in keeping with the carefree hours spent outdoors. Placemats are a more laid-back approach than tablecloths, but they follow the lead of the dishes and other accoutrements. If everything else is formal, they can certainly take on a formal tone. Setting the table with cloth napkins tells your guests that this is a special evening, and they give you the opportunity to use napkin rings, which are like jewelry for the table.

Using contrasting or comple-mentary colors or patterns among dishes and placemats or tablecloths is a good strategy. For example, if you have plain solid-colored dishes, you could opt for more colorful, patterned materials elsewhere on the table.

gallery

dishware

1 Blue-and-white china is traditional in style, elevating a meal outdoors to a special occasion.

2 A stack of the same dishes in different hues is a great way to add color to the table.

3 Square plates lend a modern flair to this English-garden–style table setting.

4 Bamboo plates are not only hip, but they're eco-friendly and durable.

5 This dinnerware has the look of ceramic, but is made of melamine, which is a scratch-resistant, durable resin.

6 Dishwasher-safe, this polycarbonate drinkware looks like clear glass but is more suited for outdoors because it's shatterproof.

LEFT It's all about the presentation. Café lights, a jaunty red lantern, and an irresistible table make casual foods and dishware more festive. Here, the hosts opted for durable ceramic dishes, real silverware, and pretty paper napkins.

•dishware

Bone china has its place on the dining table, but is probably more appropriate indoors. Eating outdoors puts tableware through the paces. Metal, melamine, and other plastic dishes are hard to break, even if they're dropped onto a concrete patio. Even ceramic can be super sturdy: Look for those labeled "high-fired" or "vitrified."

Opting for durable doesn't necessarily mean you can only do casual outside. Some styles veer more toward the formal and are perfect for special gatherings. For example, traditional patterns and sleek modern silhouettes are now sold in hard-to-break materials like plastic. Even sturdy plain white plates can adopt a fancy demeanor when the food is spectacular.

You also want to choose plates that wash up easily, namely in the dishwasher, so that outdoor entertaining isn't always accompanied by an hour-long session at the sink.

More about...
DISPOSABLE DISHES

The ultimate in convenience is the disposable dish. Of course there are the old reliables sold in the grocery store that don't have much pizzazz but get the job done. But there is also an abundance of elaborate designer paper napkins, paper plates, paper cups, and plastic plates and cups.

When you're entertaining a crowd, the ease of simply throwing away the mess is such a plus. And colorful florals or themed patterns elevate them from lowly disposable to beautiful tableware that you actually love. They allow you to retain the integrity of a special occasion while making setup and cleanup easier on the hosts.

More about...
ECO-FRIENDLY PICNICWARE

If you don't want to be adding more waste to our ever-expanding landfills, you can reduce your trash with plates, cups, and utensils made of biodegradable materials. New products are made from corn, potato, sugarcane, or soy. Oftentimes the parts of those plants that are used to make the products would otherwise be discarded.

There are even utensils that look as if they're plastic but are "bioplastic," which is made from some of those same crops. If you're super eco-diligent, some of these products can be tossed into your compost heap for quick decomposition.

TOP LEFT
Smooth black stones set in water in a large glass bowl makes for a sophisticated, organic-style centerpiece, with matching stones on each plate as place cards (write guests' names on each in white paint pen).

TOP RIGHT
A planted centerpiece, like this collection of small succulents, will last beyond the meal itself.

BOTTOM
Centerpieces needn't be confined to a container. Here, a bed of moss topped with pink roses, hydrangea, and pillar candles acts as a table runner.

CENTERPIECES WITH STYLE

One of the easiest ways to dress up the table is with a beautiful centerpiece. It allows you to celebrate the season with plants and flowers that are at their best at any given time of year. For example, a bunch of daffodils cut from the yard and placed on the table definitely lets you know it's spring.

But every centerpiece needn't be cut flowers; it can be a potted plant or a bowl of fruit or tiny ornaments. You can get creative to go with the theme of your gathering (little paper flags for the Fourth of July, for example). Just be sure that it's low enough that people can converse without it getting in their way. Or remove it from the table when everyone sits down to the meal.

LEFT A low cluster of blue hydrangea is elegantly soft, as are the lightly tinted glasses and votives. The mirrored vase reflects and repeats the tender palette.

BELOW A collection of flameless pillar candles powered by batteries looks astonishingly real but won't fall victim to a gust of wind.

ABOVE An earthenware vase filled with a cluster of grasses is a simple yet modern homage to the surrounding landscape.

LEFT A centerpiece of fresh produce is as beautiful as a bouquet of flowers and edible to boot.

lighting

● ● ● LIGHTING AN OUTDOOR DINING ROOM IS TRICKY BECAUSE OF LOGISTICS (where to hang the fixture?) and because of ambience (too much light can spoil the mood). If you have a pergola, tree, or other structure above your dining table, you can suspend an overhead fixture from it. There are many new products to choose from but if you fall in love with an old chandelier or other indoor light fixture, make sure there's overhead protection from weather and that you clean it and maintain it well.

If your dining space is out in the open, there are many ways to add subtle lighting without overpowering the space. Light up the trunk of a tree (aka "uplighting"), for example, to create the impression of light spilling down. Or put lights in the tree, for a softer moonlight effect.

When you're entertaining, sometimes the best lighting is candles: Votives cast a warm glow, and they don't take up a lot of space. Pillars add an architectural element, with their hefty, sometimes portly stature. Floating candles scream "party," as the flame flickers on the water, reflecting the light. Torches can be pushed into the ground to mark the perimeter of the party or to light a path from one spot to another.

A small outdoor pendant lamp is suspended from a tree and works in tandem with light spilling out from inside the kitchen and from along the exterior wall.

gallery

lighting options

1 A decorative metal chandelier holds candles, as does a lantern on the table, for subtle illumination.

2 The juxtaposition of rusticity and elegance: A beautiful chandelier with small shades is in keeping with the more formal oriental rug and stone statuary.

3 A pergola provides a great opportunity to hang a light over the dining table, without obstructing the view of the stars.

4 A lantern-style electric wall sconce provides enough light for the dining table.

5 String lights add to the mystique of this assemble-it-yourself pergola.

outdoor living rooms

• • •

AN OUTDOOR LIVING ROOM SHOULD BE A FULL SENSORY EXPERIENCE.
Whether it's a formal space with a couch, arm chairs, and a coffee table, or just a
hammock set up on the patio, it's an opportunity to live amid nature, with all of the
attendant sights, smells, and sounds.

The best of indoor living can be had outside, and then some. You can have all
the benefits of new technology and the latest products, juxtaposed with the age-old
beauty of Mother Nature. You can watch TV and sit by the fire, or you can play a
game of basketball or a few rounds on your putting green. The focus can be physical
activity or relaxation, a hub of energy or an escape.

What determines how you appoint your outdoor living room is how you plan to
use it. Perhaps you will have friends over for a glass of wine in the evening by the
outdoor fire pit, or maybe the neighborhood kids will stop by to play every afternoon
after school. Will you watch TV outside? Will you gather around a fire when the sun
sets? Will you curl up with a good book, and therefore need good lighting and a
soft, comfy chair? The choices may seem endless, but as you
determine how and why you want to live outdoors, your living
room will soon take shape.

This living room is so livable, with comfy teak furniture and a gas fireplace, that you might forget you're actually outside. Subtle green touches connect its surroundings: grass between the pavers, a garden, and walls of trees all around.

finding a
focal point

● ● ● TACKLE THE DESIGN OF YOUR OUTDOOR SPACE as you would an indoor space, using basic principles of interior design on the exterior. One approach is to find a focal point, which is the place to which your eyes are drawn. It could be an expansive view of a lake or a grand fireplace. Even some beautiful tiles on the rise of nearby steps can serve as a focal point.

Another design technique is to establish an "anchor," which serves as a messenger of what the space offers. For example, a tree set in the middle of a deck is one way to use living things as architectural elements, to remind you that you're outside to marvel at nature.

The fireplace is the focal point in this Phoenix-area covered patio, but the views of the desert on either side catch the eye, too. The recessed lighting over the fireplace makes the hearth stand out nicely against the dusky sky.

ABOVE Even when seating is arranged around a fireplace, making it the focus of the room, astonishing views can steal the show. And using glass or plexi walls to enclose an outdoor living area keeps the winds at bay.

RIGHT Framing a vista with trees and plantings draws the eye to the composition in the distance. Here, a single chair on a Dublin Cobbler paver patio takes advantage of the scenery.

Zesty Lemon Olives

by Ruth Lively

Lemon and herbs turn ordinary olives into something special. Make a batch or two of these ahead to have on hand when guests drop by; they'll keep in the refrigerator for a few weeks.

Yields 1 pint.

1 pint oil- or brine-packed olives, green or black or a mix
¼ teaspoon kosher salt
½ teaspoon black peppercorns
3 bay leaves
Several sprigs of rosemary or thyme
½ teaspoon fennel seeds, lightly crushed
4 or 5 cloves garlic, cut in half lengthwise
Big pinch dried red pepper flakes (optional)
2 medium lemons
3 tablespoons extra-virgin olive oil

If using brine-packed olives, drain them. In a medium bowl, combine the olives, salt, peppercorns, bay leaves, herb sprigs, fennel seeds, garlic, and red pepper flakes, if using. Zest the lemons in whatever size zest you like: a mix of finely grated zest for the brightest flavor and larger strips for color is nice. Add the zest and oil to the olives and mix well. Pour and scrape into a covered jar and refrigerate overnight to let the flavors mingle before serving.

From *Fine Cooking* 55, pp. 18

creating a conversation space

●●● IF THE FURNITURE CREATES AN ENVIRONMENT CONDUCIVE TO TALKING, your guests will fall into conversations easily, which makes for really successful parties. The chairs can be placed in a symmetrical pattern to set a more formal tone, or they can be placed purposefully to look more random. They can be clustered into pairs, or set in big groups. They should be close enough that you won't have to shout, but far enough apart that you won't feel like you're on top of one another.

Be conscious of the traffic pattern as well, placing furniture so it does not become an obstruction for people walking by, but also draws people into the space. Also make sure there's enough open area around each chair to allow easy coming and going.

**RIGHT If you
entertain frequently,
it makes sense to
keep portable seating
on hand. These
poufs are light and
along with cushioned
window-seating,
create a conversation
space on the spot.**

FACING PAGE
**A Louisiana covered
porch with antique
pine beams is
designed with
conversation in
mind. The interior
living room opens
onto this outdoor
space, so that when
the homeowners
entertain, there's
an easy flow
between the two.**

ABOVE **The contemporary
fire pit is the focal point in this
concrete conversation space, but
the intimate scale makes the tête-
a-tête the draw. The surrounding
foliage make it feel even cozier.**

More about...
FURNITURE
ARRANGEMENTS

he spacing of furniture can set the tone for
your space. Here, are some basics to keep
in mind:

• Sketch out the layout of your outdoor living room
on graph paper, using 1 inch on the paper for every
1 foot in reality. This way you can approximate the
size of the furniture you will need. But be flexible:
Once you get the furniture, you'll need to see how it
feels and make adjustments.

• Determine your traffic-flow patterns by looking
at all entrances and exits to the room. Keep seating
and other furniture clear of the path from one exit or
entrance to another. You don't want the path to go
right through the middle of the conversation, or for
people to have to move every time someone wants
to get by.

• Chairs should be a foot away from the coffee
table, to allow for easy reaching for your drink but so
that there's still room for legs. Also allow extra space
for additional seating if you entertain frequently.

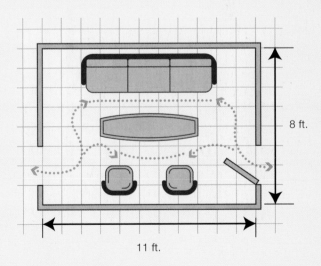

8 ft.

11 ft.

LEFT Pine beams, old brick, and a covered patio fitted with a kitchen provide a solid architectural presence and protection from the rain.

FACING PAGE Overflowing ferns mark the entrance to this graceful backyard tent. It's an asset for a family that entertains often, since they don't have to cancel in inclement weather.

BELOW An inexpensive alternative to a fixed awning or tent is a shade sail made of all-weather knit fabric that can be stretched overhead.

LEFT Just outside the house, this awning-covered deck has the best of indoors (with protection from weather) and the best of outdoors (with fresh air and garden views).

• tents and awnings

Providing coverage overhead serves many purposes for an outdoor space. Even without walls on all sides, a living room can feel more like an actual room when you give it a ceiling. It defines the area, without closing it in.

Awnings and tents also protect you from the weather, so you can take advantage of your outdoor living room even when it's raining. They can be attached to the house, or freestanding; retractable or permanent. You can purchase one that is prefabricated, or have one designed specially for your space. Look for weather-resistant and fade-resistant materials so that its life span will be extended. Retractable styles will last even longer, since you can tuck them away when not in use.

BELOW Surrounded by plants and trees, this outdoor living space is defined by a pergola that has "living" posts covered in crawling vines. Sitting here, the only break from the green is through the top of the structure, where the sky is partitioned into squares.

RIGHT Much less expensive than building a pool house, erecting a pavilion on the deck of a pool offers the same comforts and elegance. This one is made of durable cast aluminum and rolled tubular steel, and has a retractable mildew-resistant, UV-treated fabric awning.

•trellises and pergolas

Like tents and awnings, trellises and pergolas provide definition for a space, establishing it as a room. But they are more open and allow for more visibility of nature and the surroundings. They can be made of wood, stone, all-weather fiberglass, metal, or any other durable, weather-resistant material. Oftentimes vines and other plants climb their openwork, creating an atmosphere even more intimate with nature. Some are freestanding, others are attached to the house; some are fixed in a lawn, others are placed on a paved or stone surface.

The style you choose can really set the mood in your yard and tie in with the architecture of your home. For example, one with grand, round columns would carry the formality into the garden, while one with a pagoda-style top might work well with a home or garden that incorporates Asian designs.

TOP LEFT AND RIGHT You can buy powder-coated wire structures in various sizes to create decidedly different results. A small one can be a quiet respite on a garden path; a large one can be adorned with curtains to turn a field into a room.

BELOW A patio becomes a bona fide room with an airy white pergola and railing to delineate it. The sunshine filtering through the slats casts interesting shadows on the walls. Wall art and a large mirror further establish it as an extension of home.

creating discrete spaces

● ● ● THE CHALLENGE OF TURNING AN EXPANSE OF YARD INTO A SERIES OF ROOMS and spaces is to do so subtly, without erecting walls for each or cordoning them off. You don't want to create a restrictive feeling that's contrary to the freedom of outdoor living. Instead, establish enough openness that people can move freely between one room and the next, but with enough of a distinction that the purpose for each is clear.

Using different flooring materials and patterns, a variety of elevations for the rooms, and subtle changes in plant materials are just some of the ways to indicate you've entered a new "room." At night, a change in lighting can also help make one space feel separate from another.

FACING PAGE
These outdoor rooms are defined without walls. Steps up to the living room separate it from the dining room and kitchen. Pergolas and different floor patterns further distinguish the various spaces.

ABOVE How and when you use a space will dictate when you'll desire shade or sunshine. Here, the dining table is situated so that at the right time of day, it's bathed in sunlight; later, it will be the two chairs' turn.

RIGHT Walls and a freestanding roof help set off the dining area and kitchen from the pool deck. A fireplace serves as the anchor of the living space; the pool itself is the anchor of the deck. All is unified with flagstone flooring.

maximizing seating

● ● ● MAKING THE MOST OF YOUR SEATING SPACE IS ESSENTIAL to good entertaining. One of the best ways to do so is with built-in seating, which can function as an architectural element, as well as a place to rest.

Built-in seating can be soft, with a tailor-made cushion and pillows, or more structural, made of concrete or even sod. It can blend in, so that you don't even realize the spot is intended for seating, or it can be very clearly for that purpose, with pillows and throws. It can be part of a retaining wall or planter designed with a broad ledge, or it can be steps that are expansive enough to sit on. Just be sure that if you're using a stone material that it's not jagged; it needs to be smooth enough to sit on with bare legs.

ABOVE
A contemporary concrete bench mirrors the curves of the fire pit. Both feel of-the-earth because of the clean lines and simple material. And with the addition of a few clusters of throw pillows, it becomes a welcoming space.

RIGHT
The same techniques for maximizing seating inside apply outdoors too. Namely, ottomans that can slide under a coffee table can be pulled out for large gatherings. If you need extra serving space as well, place a tray on top of one to transform it into another side table.

This built-in corner bench serves as the boundary for the room, and provides a deliciously comfortable spot to seat a handful of guests. The soft palette relates well with the blue sky, and establishes a tropical ambience that's reiterated by the palm trees in the distance.

SEATING AS PART OF THE LANDSCAPE

One of the most subtle, creative ways to add seating is to take advantage of the landscape of your yard. You could use planters with deep tops as places for children to perch with their plates—a very special kids' table created in scale with their bodies.

It's an exciting treat for a child to dine below the potted plant, and it makes for easy cleanup for you.

You can also design steps to be deep enough that they can function as seating. Or a low retaining wall can double as a bench when guests outnumber more traditional seats. Some other great options: boulders, mounds, and ledges.

Using natural elements such as these invites people to sit down whenever the mood grabs them, and makes them feel at ease.

ABOVE When your entire yard has a great view, design the steps with a deeper tread to accommodate seating. Seats are comfortable when they're about 18 inches tall and 18 inches deep.

RIGHT Using boulders as seating is a naturalistic solution. For ample space, you want one that is about 2 feet by 3 feet minimum. The top can be practically flat, as shown here. Or it can look more like a natural rock formation. Just be sure it is smooth enough for comfortable sitting.

FACING PAGE This half-circle sod "sofa" is a great way to take advantage of a sloped property. The contour was manipulated, graded, and planted. With the quick addition of some throw pillows and a coffee table, it's dressed up for a party.

decorating
without walls

●●● NOT HAVING WALLS MAY SEEM LIKE AN OBSTACLE TO BE OVERCOME when you're thinking about decorating your outside space, but it's actually a perk: The view can provide all of the visual stimulation you need. You can use structures like pergolas and porch posts to frame these views, making them a living, breathing piece of art. Arches add soft curves and, when covered in climbing vines or flowering plants, a focal point above. Don't forget about the beauty of the sky as well, since a living space with an open or partially open structure overhead can bring an entirely new dimension and palette to the mix.

Even without a magnificent view, the colors and textures of nature make a wonderful tapestry. It's like incorporating Mother Nature's handiwork into your own décor. You can supplement with complementary artwork, furniture, and pillows, but the star of the show is usually what lies just beyond the living room itself.

A gas fireplace warms the already stunning view from this outdoor living room, with an infinity-edge pool that blends seamlessly with the bay in the distance.

LEFT A beautiful flowering garden serves as one wall—with all-natural floral "wallpaper"—in this tailored yet casual living room. An attractive heat lamp makes it useful, even when the weather turns chillier.

ABOVE A built-in bench acts as a barrier along the lip of this deck, but with discrete legs, it looks more like a piece of freestanding furniture. The deck is accessible through French doors that open out from a bedroom, and is an ideal gathering space for parties.

decorating with walls

●●● ENCLOSED OUTDOOR ROOMS PROVIDE YOU WITH THE WALLS AND SPACE to hang artwork, light fixtures, and anything else you want. But keep in mind that it's nice to have the beauty of nature make an appearance through glass walls, large windows, or one open wall, which can be cordoned off with curtains. If you're adding on and want to make the new space look as if it's always been there, stay true to the architecture and materials of the home.

Having walls also gives you more flexibility when it comes to furnishings, which are going to suffer less wear and tear when protected from the elements.

BELOW Stucco walls and a ceiling with interesting rustic beams give this outdoor living room a polished look. Built-in shelving, a tile fireplace surround, and on one wall, drapes all lend an air of refinement.

LEFT
This glassed-in sunroom marries the best of outdoors and in. The exposed brick wall and matching floor, along with the topiary and plant-filled urns, give it a decidedly garden feel. The caned chairs, gilded mirror, and rich wood furniture provide a refinement to balance it out.

ABOVE For the outdoor living room of a mid-century modern home, maintaining the integrity of the materials is essential. Everything here has clean lines, to allow those materials to shine. The frosted Lucite half-wall hugs one side and the corners, letting plenty of light come through but providing ample privacy from the street below.

choosing furniture

● ● ● THESE DAYS, FURNITURE STYLES RANGE FROM SPARE WROUGHT IRON TO CUSHION-LADEN TEAK. Many manufacturers have come out with styles that would look as much at home inside as they do outside: overstuffed cushions, full sofas, sectionals, even recliners. Most styles are metal, wicker, plastic, wood, or a combination thereof.

Aesthetics aside, you should consider your lifestyle in order to pick what best suits you. If you live in a temperate climate and won't be able to use your outdoor room year-round, think about choosing something that either can stay out all winter (like cast iron) or something that can easily be put away in storage until the following season. And look for cushions made of weather-resistant fabrics like polyester, and materials that are UV-resistant so they won't fade.

RIGHT
When choosing furnishings, consider the setting. Here, the mountain vista takes the stage, thanks to the uncluttered look and earthy colors of the contemporary furniture.

FACING PAGE BOTTOM
Resin wicker imitates the look of vintage, but resists heat, moisture, cracking, and fading. The frames of the chairs are lightweight but sturdy, and they won't rust. The aged zinc table will darken over time, giving it a vintage look as well.

LEFT Today's wicker is often more durable and weather resistant, but antique wicker has a rustic character that is virtually impossible to replicate.

BELOW Matching wicker chairs and fire pit give a room a happy cohesiveness. The gas fire pit doubles as a coffee table, with its black glass top.

• wicker and rattan

Perhaps the most historical of outdoor furniture, wicker is made of woven grasses, wood, paper, or even plastic. The woven technique dates to ancient times, but wicker isn't always old-fashioned in appearance. Many styles have been reinvented for the modern eye, with more sophisticated silhouettes and a wider selection of colors. Because wicker has openings between each strand that is woven, there's more surface area that can become dirty. To clean, all you need to do is wipe it down with a damp rag (and soap and water if it's made of more durable materials like resin).

• metal

When it comes to outdoor furniture, metal is one of the most durable options but can also be quite expensive. This category includes aluminum, iron (cast and wrought), and steel. Some styles feature hollow tubing, others are solid. You want something sturdy enough to withstand a stiff wind but light enough to be moved easily.

Aluminum and steel can take on a decidedly modern look, while wrought iron tends toward the more traditional, as in an English garden style. You'll find aluminum is often powder coated, which means the paint is applied using electrical charges and then is baked on for increased durability.

FACING PAGE Lightweight metal pool furnishings like these are durable enough to stay put with a gust of wind but light enough to take inside after the season has come to a close.

BELOW Heavyweight wrought-iron chairs, made delicate with curlicue arms and wrought semicircles underneath, are further softened by extra-thick cushions.

More about...
METAL FURNITURE

aluminum: Most popular because it resists rust and corrosion. But it can become quite hot, so be careful if you're sitting with bare legs. It can either be "cast aluminum," which means it was formed using a mold. Or it can be "tubular" or hollow aluminum, which, because it's not solid, is not as durable. It's easy to pick up, though, so is great for seasonal furnishings that need to be stowed away.

Wrought iron: This is a traditional garden furniture material, and it's heavy. This might not seem like a problem if you intend to keep the furniture outside year-round, but keep in mind that it can sink into a grassy lawn, or crack stone flooring because of its weight. And make sure to waterproof your wrought iron so it won't rust.

Stainless steel: The name isn't completely accurate, because stainless can rust if you don't care for it properly. Be sure to clean off spills or pollen right away.

More about... BALAU

balau is the poor man's teak, but it's beautiful and rich-looking nonetheless. Balau is a more affordable option than teak, for a similar look and durability. In fact, it's actually denser than teak, so it's no surprise that it's often used for industrial purposes, like on bridges and ships.

Because it's an oily wood, it doesn't dry out; and it's weather, critter, and mildew resistant. Its color is a slightly warmer brown but it weathers to a gray color like teak. If you want it to stay brown, clean and treat it each year with a water-based sealant.

TOP A light finish on this teak furniture is a nice contrast to the dark-wood coffee table. The orange cushions are bold enough to stand out against both, yet remain soothing. The lighter-colored piping ties it all together.

MIDDLE Modular contemporary pieces of teak furniture (love seat, lounge chair, and corner seat) can be arranged in almost any configuration; clamps hold them in place.

BOTTOM This teak furniture set is constructed with mortise and tenon joinery to reveal a true craftsmanship.

Splashes of color are invigorating, thanks to the cherry red pillows, in an otherwise subdued color palette. The teak seating matches the teak fire pit.

• wood

Wood tends to be less expensive than metal but can rot over time if not properly cared for. It mimics the appearance of nature, since it actually originates from trees like the ones growing in your yard. Teak is one of the most popular choices, because it's a naturally oily wood and stands up well. But it can be quite pricey and will age to a silvery gray. If you don't like the weathered look, you'll need to sand and oil it every year.

Other options include balau and jatoba (aka Brazilian cherry), which are also durable tropical woods, but are less expensive. These teak alternatives can be cared for with many of the same products; the difference is that jatoba ages to a deep reddish color instead of gray. Because of the demand for teak, it is being harvested faster than it can be replenished. But all tropical woods are a precious resource whose harvesting can greatly damage rain forests, so to be eco-friendly, look for those certified by the Forest Stewardship Council as having been sustainably harvested.

• plastic

Banish the mental image you may have of cheap, flimsy plastic lawn chairs. There's a new breed of lawn furniture out there, which means there's a lot to choose from when it comes to plastic or plastic-coated furniture. Look for terms like *vinyl* and *resin*, both of which are just different ways to say plastic. Recycled plastic is perhaps the best option, since it puts materials to use that otherwise would wind up in landfills. It can contain everything from empty yogurt cups to spent laundry detergent bottles to old plastic furniture.

The big benefit of plastic furniture is if your room is exposed to the weather, it fares well. The same reason environmentalists don't want plastic in landfills—because it takes thousands of years to decompose, if ever—is why it makes for durable outdoor furniture. Plus, it's easy to clean with just a hose, especially if you rinse it off immediately after you spot food and pollen stains. Lighter plastic pieces also make the ritual transport of furniture from outdoors to in and back out again much less of a strain on your back.

Plastic-coated lime-green cushions with dark piping are bright and cheery in this retro living space. The cushions are easy to care for, and can be wiped down with just mild soap and a damp cloth.

LEFT
Black polyethylene is woven over tubular aluminum frames on these adjoined chairs. The sophisticated green and black cushions are elegantly accented by the floral rug and silver furniture legs.

BELOW
Bright yellow molded plastic brings out the sun even on an overcast day. It's a perfect conversation cluster for an urban rooftop.

flooring

● ● ● A CLOSE LOOK AT THE FLOOR OF AN OUTDOOR ROOM WILL TELL YOU A LOT. For a more traditional space, oftentimes a uniform rectangular stone pattern called ashlar is used. In between the stones can be grout, gravel, or plant material. Brick or concrete pavers made to look like stone or brick also telegraph a more formal space. For more casual areas, you will want random patterns of round or amorphous stones, called as a category "flagstone" or simply "flags."

For safety's sake, avoid glazed or porous tiles or stone because they can become slippery when wet.

RIGHT Tumbled pavers with edges that look hand-hewn can be stone, or concrete made to look like stone. The pavers in this dining area line up in concentric circles but end at a lighter colored border made up of larger pavers, much like an area rug.

More about...
BLUESTONE

bluestone is a type of sandstone that isn't always blue. It comes in a variety of colors, including green, yellow, purple, and gray. Popular because it's easy to cut and wears well, bluestone is not only great for floors, but for walls, countertops, and other architectural elements.

Because it's comprised of layers of sediment, it does tend to flake. But you needn't worry unless large chunks start coming off, at which time the entire piece could crack and require replacement. Bluestone can be quite pricey, so you may consider the less-expensive alternative of concrete pavers made to look like bluestone.

FACING PAGE A change in flooring is a subtle way to indicate a special border. Here, the brick flooring in this Louisiana home undergoes a distinct change as it moves from the covered patio to the pool deck, where the running bond pattern is further broken up with soft grass.

LEFT Playing with stone and grass patterns is a dynamic approach to building a pathway. Here, stone and grass cutouts create a geometric puzzle and add tremendous interest to the lawn.

LEFT Wood decking can be upgraded with paint and a ruler or stencil. The black-and-white diamond pattern plays off of the checked seat cushions and napkins, and adds length to the space. Be sure to coat the painted deck with a good-quality deck sealer to prolong its life; repaint it every couple of years.

ABOVE Subtle distinctions in floor patterns can reveal volumes about the use of the space. As this floor moves from the living room to an area with a spa, it goes from the more formal ashlar pattern of rectangles to the random flagstone pattern. The latter is more casual, hence the plant growth between the stones.

LEFT A beautiful wood deck adds texture and richness, thanks to its natural variegation. The goal is to show off the integrity of the material, so it has to be refinished and sealed every other year.

FACING PAGE A honey-colored pattern of random shaped stone is transected by darker pavers that lead to a stone compass before the fireplace, a nautical homage at this seaside retreat.

More about...
CONCRETE FLOORS

oncrete is the chameleon of floor materials. It can be made to mimic a variety of real stones, like cobblestone and bluestone, and is much less expensive but still quite strong.

Concrete can also be designed to look like actual tile pavers. It can be stamped to create patterns or treated with acid or water-based stains to bring out a mottled look. The options with concrete are endless, and can be customized to your exact specifications.

• patterned floors

Sometimes homeowners opt for a plain floor, so that the furniture and the other elements of the room really stand out, or because the architecture of the home is also minimalist. But the opposite strategy is just as appealing: to turn the floor into a showpiece of its own.

Patterns can be worked into the flooring in myriad ways. A pattern can be the result of the natural variations within a particular material, like the streaks in an exotic wood, or because of paint or stain applied to the surface. Patterning can also be achieved by arranging different-colored materials side by side, creating an arresting contrast. For example, red brick flooring with light-colored concrete accents.

Even monochromatic pavers—which are rectangular stones, tiles, or concrete—can take on a design. For example, lining them up so that all of their ends are exactly even is called "stack bond"; "running bond" is where a brick is set so that its end is in the middle of the brick below it. Other patterns include herringbone, basketweave, and pinwheel.

finishing touches

● ● ● AN OUTDOOR LIVING ROOM SHOULD BE SO COMFORTABLE that you want to spend all your time there. So it's important to decorate it to feel as much like home as the indoor living room does. A sparsely decorated space can be uninviting and actually make you use the room less frequently.

No detail is too small when it comes to making an outdoor living room just right. Using rugs, pillows, throws, lamps, artwork, and all the other niceties can set the style, put you at ease, and in effect, result in an addition to your home. Perhaps best of all, decorating this way gives you permission to spend more time outside.

TOP This Turkish-pattern reversible all-weather rug is made from recycled plastic soda bottles, making it good-looking and good for the earth. It may look too nice to hose down, but that's all you need to do to clean it.

RIGHT Floor pillows in weather- and UV-resistant fabrics are ideal for party-throwing. They're instant seating and hardy enough to take on the task.

ABOVE The growing selection of outdoor fabrics and pillows that are weather-resistant means new decorating options, like these Batik-style polyester outdoor throw pillows.

LEFT Some outdoor rugs are made of synthetics that are quick-drying, weather-resistant, and super-durable, but have the look of natural materials like jute or sisal. Just spray down with a hose to clean and enjoy.

• rugs, pillows, and throws

These are usually the stuff of indoor living, but durable, water-resistant fabrics and a bevy of styles make it possible to carry your personal aesthetic outside. Rugs you can put outdoors can be made of man-made materials, like DuraCord®, or natural materials, like bamboo or coir. Look for ones that are mildew resistant and colorfast, so they won't fade in the sun.

Outdoor pillows made of weather-resistant fabrics like Sunbrella® come in all manner of patterns and colors, so you have the same selection you're accustomed to when you decorate indoors. They are mildew resistant, but still shouldn't be left out in the rain uncovered.

Keeping a few throw blankets outside is ideal for when the sun sets and there's a chill in the air. Just be sure to choose ones made of a washable, colorfast material. And when you're done, stow them away in a cabinet or other protected storage area.

When an abundance of flowering plants don't bring color to your living space, you can rely on rugs and pillows. Here, the earthy tones of an adobe-style home get a wakeup call from Southwestern yellows, oranges, and reds.

lighting

●●● THE POPULARITY OF OUTDOOR LIVING
has led to newer and more attractive lighting options for
outdoor spaces. Overhead fixtures and even chandeliers are available for
outdoor use, both electric and gas powered, if you have a ceiling to
work with.

Even if you don't, you can place lights in a tree to shine down as if
moonlight, or place them on the ground to highlight your landscape features.
A ground light directed at a beautiful old oak, for example, will illuminate the
lacy silhouette and will spill over into the living space, creating an indirect
but still useful glow. To achieve more subtle lighting, you can replace every
one 20-watt light bulb with two that are 10 watts each. This better
disperses the light but gives you the same total number of watts.

A large covered porch in southern Virginia is the perfect setting for quiet conversation. The lantern-style sconces and suspended fixtures echo the light pouring in through the doors to softly illuminate the oversized space.

LEFT The style of your fixtures can amplify the style of your home. Here, a streetlamp-style light draws attention to the detailed corbels above and below the balcony.

BOTTOM LEFT Candlelight always casts a warm glow, which is great for entertaining. Clusters of these outdoor lanterns can be hung from chains or set on the table. Each one holds three votive candles or one larger pillar. They're stainless steel made to look like copper.

BOTTOM RIGHT With a fire pit as the focal point of this space, the fire itself provides ample illumination for those gathered around. Additional fixtures nearby amply light the pathway.

RIGHT A table lamp especially made for outdoor living is just one of the small details that makes this room feel homey.

BOTTOM LEFT Somehow string lights always make a party feel more festive. They can be attached under an eave, through a plant or topiary, or woven between the spokes of an outdoor umbrella.

BOTTOM RIGHT These gas-powered lanterns provide a flame that will run for 15 hours on their lightweight 1-pound tanks.

• lighting you can move

Some outdoor living rooms don't have any walls or ceilings for light fixtures, but there are plenty of options to accommodate that. Table and floor lamps are available for outdoor use, and come with weather-resistant fabric shades and encased lightbulbs that prevent water from getting in.

There are contemporary and traditional, formal and casual options, depending on the mood you want to set. For instance, string lights can be hung in a tree overhead to add a casual starlight twinkle. And, of course, votive candles add a romantic glow.

• heaters

In many parts of the country when fall and winter settle in, people retreat indoors. But because patio heaters can warm up a sizable space (20 to 25 feet away), the party can continue well into the colder months.

There are several outdoor heating options: Some are small rectangular units fixed to the wall under eaves or beams, and radiate the heat downward. Others are freestanding lamppost-esque furnishings that sit on the floor or a table and can be moved around. Most of the freestanding ones are powered by liquid propane; the wall-mounted ones are either electric or natural gas. Perhaps the most extravagant and comfortable option is installing radiant heat under the floors (and even the countertops), so that wherever you go outside, your feet remain nice and toasty.

LEFT This heat lamp blends nicely with its surroundings, sporting some healthy curves. Even the "lid" on top is bowl-shaped, for a softness that mimics the curlicues of the furniture.

MIDDLE A patio heater blends into the environs because it has the look of a sleek stainless lamp. It's also being used to distract from the speaker mounted just above. This model has a built-in side table, a great resting spot for drinks and a handy storage cabinet.

BOTTOM Wall-mounted heaters are a great option if you have limited floor space or need it in a high-traffic area where it could be knocked over or obstruct a pathway. A space heater tucked under an eave keeps this California pool house warm throughout the year.

OUTDOOR ARTWORK

hanging artwork may seem the domain of interior living rooms, but there is a plethora of paintings, sculpture, and other masterpieces that would thrive outside. If your outdoor living room does have walls, they are almost asking for adornment. Doing so provides color year-round, regardless of what the garden is doing. It also adds interest to the space, and can even be a focal point for the whole room.

If you like the colors of a particular piece, you can incorporate those into your furnishings, just as you would indoors. And check with your local art shop to see if they can transfer a print to canvas using waterproof inks. Or you can buy artwork specifically designed for outdoors, like those from openairdesigns.com.

TOP On this outdoor fireplace, the mantel shows off souvenirs from around the world. Exotic elephant statues flank a rustic wood-framed mirror.

RIGHT Even when the space is flooded with light, this mirror is working hard to bring in more greenery from the garden. When the fire is roaring at night, the mirror takes a backseat to the beauty of the flames.

TOP Creating a delightful vignette can be a powerful focal point. Here, a terra-cotta bas relief is surrounded by pale apricot roses, shrimp plants, flax, and sedum. The homeowner has also added a personal touch—her favorite marbles.

BOTTOM A covered porch is an ideal spot for a favorite oil painting (taken in during the winter months). The flower motif plays off the blooms in the nearby garden, bringing them closer to where you sit.

White Bean Artichoke Dip

by *Fine Cooking* staff

Yields 6 to 8 servings as an appetizer; about 2 cups of dip

1 can (15½ ounces) cannelloni beans, drained and rinsed
1 can (14½ ounces) artichoke hearts, drained and rinsed
1 small clove garlic, chopped
2 tablespoons fresh lemon juice
2 tablespoons extra-virgin olive oil; more for drizzling
3 tablespoons freshly grated Parmigiano Reggiano
1 teaspoon chopped fresh rosemary
Kosher salt and freshly ground black pepper
Cayenne

In a food processor, blend the beans, artichoke hearts, garlic, and lemon juice to a smooth paste. With the machine running, add the oil. If needed, add 1 to 2 tablespoons water to get a smooth consistency. Blend in the cheese and rosemary; season with salt and pepper. Transfer to a medium bowl, sprinkle with 2 generous pinches cayenne and drizzle with oil. Serve with crackers or pita chips.

Make Ahead Tip

You can make the dip a day ahead and refrigerate it; bring it to room temperature before serving.

From *Fine Cooking* 51, pp. 86B

outdoor entertainment

●●● TVS AREN'T JUST FOR INDOORS ANYMORE. These days, some are made of weather-resistant materials, and can join you in an outdoor room or even by the pool. Some are fixed to a wall; others are freestanding units; some are even inflatable. They come with all the bells and whistles, like attachments for a DVD player or an mp3 player, and remote controls that can also be hooked up to adjust your pool or spa functions.

If you don't want to make the big investment but still want to watch a great flick outside, you could opt to rent a DVD projector to watch a movie on a blank exterior wall. This is a great option for a movie-night theme party. Make popcorn and serve some refreshments and classic theater candies to flesh out the theme.

Sound systems are also a great entertainment option, to set the mood with the right kind of music. Many speakers aren't even visible, and can be sunk into the ground or attached to an overhead structure. Most can be controlled from indoors so the host has easy (and exclusive) access. Alternatively, some speakers are visible but portable, and many are even waterproof.

TOP LEFT This LCD outdoor wall TV is sealed inside an all-weather protective shield that keeps insects, rain, dirt, and scratches at bay.

TOP RIGHT Hiding outdoor electronic equipment is easier than you might think. Here, a speaker is installed low to the ground so that it blends in with the soil.

LEFT Covered in 16-gauge stainless steel, this futuristic-looking TV and stand is weather resistant and has marine-grade speakers so you can watch it from your pool. Now, that's luxury.

FACING PAGE This space was built with a television in mind. The alcove constructed above the fireplace allows the homeowners to turn it on while enjoying a fire or eating at the dining table.

ABOVE This outdoor unit includes a fireplace, fire pit, and even a kitchen on the opposite end. It comes equipped with a 42-inch plasma TV that rises out of the unit, so it's visible only when you want it to be.

by the fire

AN ALMOST PRIMAL URGE to connect with the most basic pleasures. So it's no wonder that many of us want or have some sort of fireplace or fire pit.

Fireplaces tend to be quiet spaces, while fire pits are intensely conversational. To figure out which is best for you, ask yourself how you and your family plan to use it.

Built-in fireplaces are often made of stainless steel, along with granite, tile, brick, or another stone facade. You can also choose between the standard wood-fueled fireplace or one that is gas-powered (which is simple to light and doesn't require logs). Or there's the combination of gas and wood, which has the best of both: the ease of gas and the appealing fragrance of wood.

FACING PAGE TOP Dufferin stone, a concrete veneer, was used to construct this pre-fabricated fireplace. A similar look for less money is available in materials from brick to stucco to stone.

FACING PAGE BOTTOM This elevated wood-burning fireplace with a convenient gas starter provides a great vantage point for enjoying the view below.

ABOVE Wide steps with flowers growing along the risers welcome all into this fireplace room. There's ample space for additional chairs, but guests can also sit on the extra-wide ledge atop the short wall.

More about... CHIMINEAS

Chimineas are a less-expensive, portable version of the outdoor fireplace, with a rusticity that makes them handsome and practical. They originated as cooking vessels in Mexican villages, where they prevented rain from extinguishing the fire.

Today, they're made mostly of copper, clay, steel, cast iron, or cast aluminum, and their most notable characteristic is the chimney-like extension from the top, which helps direct smoke away from those gathered around it.

Be sure to look for models with ample space inside, so you can use standard-size pieces of wood (otherwise you'd have to special order smaller wood or cut it down yourself). Alternatively, you can choose a model that runs on gas or propane. Above all, be sure to place your chiminea where there's no danger that anything will catch fire overhead.

LEFT Using light-colored grout on a dark stone fireplace accentuates the shape of the stone. Here, local stone was quarried for the floor to match the fireplace, which is original to the house.

BELOW The minimalist design for this space puts the architecture on display. Instead of conventional furniture, a built-in ledge on the hearth creates a cozy seat that's close to the warmth.

gallery

portable fire pits

Portable fire pits can travel with the party and allow you to maximize space and seating. There are many different styles in all price ranges. Most burn wood and charcoal, but you can also find gas-powered models. Some provide extra surface area and double as a coffee table; others are shaped like a cauldron, perfect for toasting s'mores or hotdogs. Be sure to read the instructions before using, since many can't be lit close to the house, on grass, or on a wooden deck.

1 Coffee table by day; fire pit by night.

2 Copper cauldron.

3 Fire pit with spark screen.

4 Contemporary copper design.

RIGHT Having a fire pit custom made allows you to pick the exact color combination and materials you want. Here, the pinkish local stone called Santa Barbara is replicated in the flooring and pit ledge. The black base is made of stacked ledger stone.

LEFT Sculptural inform, it's the focal point of the entire yard. The spa is immediately adjacent, so it's soothing to enjoy the warmth of the fire after a soak.

RIGHT A square fire pit with a wide stone ledge is a magical spot for a picnic at sunset where it becomes the center of the conversation.

FACING PAGE People sit around most fire pits, but with this one, people sit *in*. Reminiscent of a fire ring at camp, this interpretation is powered by gas. Two levels of seating accommodate even more, making it a cozy, fun party space.

•built-in fire pits

Nothing draws a crowd quite like a fire pit. Everyone loves a good fire, with marshmallows, hot chocolate, and of course camaraderie. Because it's open on all sides, it provides heat to people gathered all around it and facilitates conversation. Plus, it adds another hardscape element to your yard, which nicely plays off of the swaths of green from garden plantings and lawns.

Built-in fire pits can run on gas, wood, or a combination of the two, but even when they're powered by gas, they can look deceptively real, while requiring much less maintenance. They can be custom designed, built yourself, or purchased prefabricated. As for materials, you usually have a choice of brick, stone, or concrete. Be sure drainage is considered when it's installed, so that rainwater is directed away from the pit itself.

places to relax

● ● ● SOMETIMES PEOPLE JUST NEED TO RELAX, so designing a space for that purpose will pay off in the long run. After a hard day at work, a few quiet moments in the yard can be rejuvenating.

There's no one right kind of spot. It can be fully appointed with all the amenities or just a hammock spanning two trees. Think about the colors and textures of the materials you're using, keeping in mind that comfort is paramount. When choosing furniture, find something that is soft enough to relax on but stiff enough to support your back. And think about whether or not the spot is always or sometimes in the shade so you'll have a retreat from the heat.

LEFT Chaise lounges are one of the most versatile pieces of furniture for relaxing. These can be turned to face the lawn, so mom and dad can kick back while the kids play in the yard, or they can be rotated to face the pool on the other side.

BELOW Sometimes all you need to lose yourself in the moment is a couple of comfy chairs, well appointed with sumptuous cushions, and a roaring fire in the middle of the afternoon.

LEFT Getting away to relax doesn't have to mean going far. The shade from the house and the view of the green yard can be transporting. The right comfy chair with an ottoman for your feet will certainly suffice, especially if you have a cuddly pooch to keep you company.

enjoying the sights and sounds

● ● ● SOMETIMES THE BEST WAY TO RELAX is to find a place with a positive sensory atmosphere, be it a beautiful sight, a beautiful sound, or a beautiful scent. Views, of course, are humbling and inspiring, and can dramatically relax you. The same holds true for sounds of nature, like the trickling of water or the chirping of birds, so think about creating your relaxing spot near a waterfall or bird feeder.

As for scent, you can use aromatic plants in the area, like peppermint geranium. Or place scented herbs in the joints between the pavers of the flooring. Each time you walk, you'll brush the plants and release the fragrance into the air.

ABOVE This patch of relaxation was created as an in-yard retreat. The adjacent stream feeds into a pond with a gentle gurgle and trickle. The surrounding sycamore and oak trees provide shade in the summer when their canopies are full.

RIGHT Located in a previously unused patch of yard, this is a treehouse for adults. The owners traveled to Bali and wanted to re-create a structure they had seen on their visit. It is built into a ledge, so it's accessible from ground level and has a panoramic view.

113

Lounge chairs take advantage of this borrowed landscape. To preserve their view, the owners installed a clear shield instead of a clunky railing, so they feel even more connected to the ocean.

places to play

● ● ● THERE'S A TIME FOR RELAXATION, AND THERE'S A TIME FOR ACTIVITY. Setting up your yard with the equipment and courts for games of all kinds is a great way for children and adults to get a little exercise and have fun. You can install many different types of sport courts in your yard: tennis, basketball, volleyball. You can even create a multipurpose surface that can be used for any and all of those.

If courts aren't your bag, consider more traditional lawn games like horseshoes, croquet, and bocce. Or maybe you'd like your very own putting green. Depending of course on your budget, an occasional hobby can become a (healthy) everyday obsession when it lands in your backyard.

Chess becomes life-size with this lawn version of the game. Red and white pavers set in grass create the board and gravel-filled areas are for keeping captured pieces.

LEFT The game of bocce is popular in Europe and especially Italy, but is growing in popularity here in the United States. Traditionally, such lawn bowling courts are made of crushed oyster shells, but you can use decomposed granite, gravel, or tennis clay, too.

BELOW If your yard isn't big enough for a full-size court, it can be proportionately adjusted. This basketball court is just under regulation size and sports outdoor court lights and an electronic scoreboard (inset).

ABOVE Hailing from Cuba, the homeowners have created the ideal spot for card games. This table features a map of that island nation in the center. When not completely captivated by the game, players can take in the stunning garden.

LEFT If the table and chairs outside this playhouse didn't provide some scale, you might think it was a charming cottage with a white picket fence.

BELOW An elaborate play structure for children features a fortress on top. There's also a tube slide, swings, a fire pole, and a climbing wall; the soft recycled-tire ground cover is eco-friendly.

•kids at play

Perhaps no activity is more appealing to a child than playing outside, especially when it involves something made just for them. This can include anything from a playhouse to a tree house to a sandbox.

It can involve sitting quietly on a special perch or descending at full speed down a slide. It can stimulate the imagination, get them moving physically, or do a little of both. You'll never again have to convince a child to go outside to play.

TOP LEFT
Covering a sandbox
with a hinged lid
keeps critters from
using it as a litter box.
For those who prefer
to watch, there's
ample seating on the
tree bench.

BOTTOM LEFT
Backyard climbing
walls offer a physical
challenge for both
kids and adults. This
one is discreetly
tucked under the
deck to make best
use of space.

ABOVE Because
this home is situated
on a steep incline,
it's difficult to access
the play area that's
well below the house.
The solution? The
children hop on the
slide at the house
and land in the grassy
play area. It's quick
transportation that is
as entertaining as it
is efficient.

by the pool

● ● ●

A DIP IN THE POOL IS ONE OF SUMMER'S GREATEST PLEASURES. Children love to splash and flip in the water, taking advantage of their weightless bodies. Adults like to cool down, relax, even swim a lap or two for exercise. Putting a pool in the backyard is a way to offer this luxury just a few steps away from the house, a wonderful treat for guests when you're entertaining outdoors.

Deciding how to add a pool to your yard takes some thought. Consider size, shape, and materials that suit your aesthetic taste, the architecture of the home, and the practical limitations of your property. If you live in a temperate climate, you probably want the pool to be in the sun, to keep the water warmer later in the day and later in the year. For more tropical areas, a shaded pool may be a welcome relief from the intense heat.

Once you have figured out all of the main design features (pool shape, decking, coping, and pool materials), move on to all of the extras: the water features, the spa, the landscaping, the lighting.

Tucked into a naturalistic setting, this amoeba-shaped pool is a wonderful spot for a party. The flagstone decking extends to the pool's edge, adding to its organic style. And the landscape of rocks and bushes further integrates it with its surroundings.

Then it's time to consider what you will use for seating around the pool. And storage: Where will you keep the pool-cleaning supplies, water toys, and seat cushions? In a pool house, a freestanding shed, or a smaller flip-lid bench? A pool is about more than swimming; it's about bringing people and nature together. It's at the heart of outdoor entertaining.

pool basics

●●● POOLS COST MONEY TO BUILD AND MAINTAIN, so it's prudent to do your homework about the best materials, shape, and measurements for your particular situation. Some homeowners want a pool that blends in with the landscape, in shape and materials; others want an architectural marvel that stands out. Some want a pool made of concrete, others want underwater tile. Some want a chlorinated pool, others may opt for saltwater. Some want lighting to emanate from inside the pool, others want lighting all around it. So there's much to consider.

The depth of the pool is also a decision waiting to be made. Most pools are 4 to 8 feet deep, but yours could be anywhere from 3 to 10 feet.

This pool takes on a more formal tone, thanks to the classic Greco-Roman shape, the fountain wall adorned with lion heads, and ornate urns filled with flowers and grasses.

CHOOSING A POOL DESIGNER

for a custom pool, a landscape architect or designer can come up with one that fits with both your home and your yard. They can help work in the landscaping and outbuildings. And they can see the project through from start to finish. If a landscape architect is out of your budget, look for a certified pool contractor. And as always, ask for references so you can see his or her handiwork. Contact a few contractors and get several different bids, so that they can compete for your business.

If you're going through a pool dealer, find out if they will actually install the pool themselves, or if they contract it out. And if they contract it out, do they still guarantee satisfaction? Also ask who will handle warranty issues that arise. Ideally the same company will manage it all so you don't run the risk of having to negotiate with several different parties.

ABOVE Blue mosaic tile is one way to bring style to your pool. Here, the tile adorns the spa and delineates the leading edge of each step for safety.

RIGHT Brick is an interesting material for decking and coping in this infinity-edge pool that appears to flow right into the Pacific Ocean. Plexiglas separates this home from the one next door so as not to obstruct the magnificent views.

pool materials

● ● ● MOST IN-GROUND POOLS ARE MADE FROM GUNITE, a sprayed-on concrete, because it's durable and easy to customize to exact specifications of your particular design. To finish the concrete, the least expensive options are paint or plaster, which are put on top. For maintenance, paint needs to be reapplied every couple of years; plaster lasts a bit longer.

A bit pricier, crushed pebbles or a concrete-quartz material is even more durable and offers a nice textured surface. The most high-end, ceramic tile is often used around the edge to dress it up, but it can also be used to cover the entire interior or to create mosaic designs on the bottom of the pool.

Other lining materials are vinyl and fiberglass, which are both prefabricated and then shipped to the site, making them more expensive than gunite. But they both require less maintenance over time (fiberglass even less than vinyl). Vinyl is popular in regions with cold weather, since it is easily winterized.

LEFT This pool interior is fiberglass, which discourages algae growth. Fiberglass also acts as an insulator, requiring less energy to heat.

FACING PAGE BOTTOM This pool was designed to look as if the house were built next to a small pond or spring. The boulders and grasses that come right up to the edge of the water add to the naturalistic composition.

LEFT A mosaic pattern of brown glass tile is organic yet sophisticated, but it's too slippery to be used where people will be walking. This type of tile is also expensive, so it's used sparingly.

BELOW The hardy Korean grass used as this pool's "decking" has an otherworldly quality to it. With its bumpy surface, it provides visual movement, texture, and interest without obstructing the view.

THE COPING

The coping around the pool, or "lip," can be made from a variety of materials. It is an opportunity to add a beautiful accent, as long as it's not slippery. A good rule of thumb is to not use more than a 2-foot-wide strip of any material because the ground invariably settles over time, which can cause cracks. So if you opt for concrete coping, don't choose solid concrete; stick with two-foot pieces mortared together.

The coping can also contribute to the style of the pool. A rolled edge, for example, provides good seating and a good grip, making it ideal for lap pools and pools where children will be playing. The cantilevered edge evokes a modern aesthetic, while the bull-nosed option is the standard classic. The rough-cut version works well in areas that have stacked stone or naturalistic settings nearby.

Coping Styles

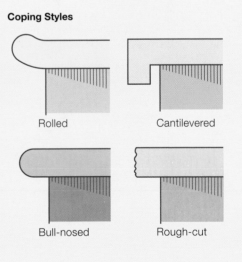

Rolled

Cantilevered

Bull-nosed

Rough-cut

deck materials

● ● ● THE AREA AROUND THE POOL, THE DECKING, utilizes a whole different set of materials. It can be concrete, wood, faux wood, grass, stone, brick, or any combination. When choosing decking material, the most important factor is slipperiness. If it gets slick when wet, it's not appropriate for the pool area, where it will often be soaked with water. And just because a stone is "porous" doesn't mean it won't be slippery. Some limestone, for example, can become quite slick. Plus, porous materials stain more easily.

There are spray products that can be applied to a pool deck to increase grip and reduce slipperiness, but they do wear away and will need to be reapplied frequently. Even after you find a material with enough traction, be sure to keep the surface clear of any moss, which can also make it slippery and dangerous.

For the decking, you also need to consider how hot it will become in the sun. Dark materials absorb heat. If you want to test how a particular material will heat up in your yard, put out a sample where the pool will eventually be installed, let it sit out in the sun for a few hours, and step on it without shoes.

Creating a stepping stone in the midst of a mosaic tile "stream" is one way to blend a pool with its natural surrounds. Here, it connects a pool and spa.

RIGHT Brick coping with a blue tile wall between the spa and pool is in keeping with the rustic elegance of this Mediterranean-style home.

More about...
POOL ACCESSORIES

With great pool fun comes basic maintenance. The water ph must be balanced, and the pool must be cleared of debris. You'll need to consider automated pool cleaners, which essentially vacuum the water; pool pumps and filters, which circulate and clean the water; chemicals, which are used to keep bacteria out; and pool heaters, which make that morning swim a lovely way to wake up. One note on heating systems: Solar pool heaters allow you to heat the pool without using any additional energy, since they are powered by the sun.

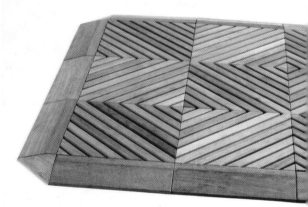

LEFT This pool deck takes on a modern, minimalist aesthetic, with large concrete slabs separated by joints of smooth gray stones. The light color means it won't heat up in the sun, and the stones allow for drainage when it rains.

ABOVE Install your own teak deck, using these 18-inch square panels that snap together with stainless-steel hardware. They can be put on top of almost any material (even crushed stone). Keep in mind that because they're teak, they will age to a weathered gray color.

pool shapes

● ● ● CHOOSING A POOL SHAPE DEPENDS ON THE LAYOUT OF YOUR

YARD and the ways in which you plan to enjoy it. Maybe you want it to appear as if it's an extension of the contour of the landscape, like part of a bay that borders your property. Or perhaps you want it to stand out, with geometric angles that create a severe contrast to the softness of nature.

Standard rectangular and symmetrical circular shapes are less expensive, as are their accessories (like pool covers). When you start getting into customized shapes, you're going to be paying to customize everything, including the pool cover.

Whatever shape you choose, you definitely want it to also look beautiful when you're looking out the window, since you'll most likely be spending more time seeing it from there than from any other spot.

This tadpole-shaped pool is ideal for taking a dip or playing around. It seems to almost hug the pool house, which is close enough that swimmers can hang out on the porch.

LEFT What appears to be an L-shaped pool is actually a rectangular lap pool adjoined with a square spa. The configuration allows the spa to be more secluded.

BELOW To make this pool feel organic, it was designed with a beach entry. To simulate the horizon of the sea, the water appears to merge with the landscape.

pool shapes

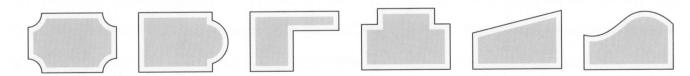

ABOVE-GROUND POOLS

above-ground pools are the red-headed stepchildren of the pool world, because, let's face it, they can be an eyesore. Many wind up looking like a large bowl that was plopped in the middle of a yard. But with a little ingenuity, you can blend them into the landscape a bit more successfully. One option is to build a deck around the pool, giving the impression that it's built into the ground by bringing the "ground" up to the pool itself. This can be done with steps and wood slatted decking, and can look quite lovely with potted plants and other landscaping around it.

The draw of the above-ground pool is that it's much less expensive than installing an in-ground pool. And if you're not committed to the idea of digging up your yard, it's a great first step, letting you figure out if a pool is the right decision for your family. It also makes a good choice if you're planning to move after a few years because you can oftentimes take it with you. That said, the lifespan of an above-ground pool isn't as great as that of an in-ground pool, so it will need to be replaced more frequently.

the right shape for your yard

Choosing a pool shape and size that fits your yard is easy if you know the formula. You need 4 or 5 feet of space on the decking so that people can pass safely back and forth from the pool. If you plan to have chaises by the pool, a 10- to 12-foot deep decking would accommodate the chairs and leave enough room to pass safely. When calculating the measurements, keep in mind that adding tables and chairs will eat into your total space as well.

The widely held rule of thumb is that a 16- by 32-foot pool provides enough space for all of the activities you could want. Small pools are popular, however, in part because they can fit on even a small patch of lawn, and no matter the size, they still satisfy the desire to take a cool dip. The other upside is that they're cheaper to heat and less work to maintain.

LEFT The shape of this pool is reminiscent of a gem: when lit up at night from underwater, it looks like a blue topaz or aquamarine. The shape also brings in an element of Art Deco, which relates well with the illuminated palm trees.

ABOVE This more traditional style of pool and deck, with the pergolas and pillars along the edge, creates an air of Italianate luxury. The rectangular pavers on the deck and rectangular steps into the pool echo the 90-degree angles of the pool.

LEFT Geometric and elongated, this pool's unique shape fits the spatial constraints of the yard while still being interesting and attractive. Each angle creates a different entry point for swimmers. And to continue the visual symmetry, sheets of water pour in from every wall facing this direction, creating a soothing sound.

This asymmetrical geometric design elicits a formal tone, further accentuated by the elevated fountain and columns. The near side is meant for sunbathers; the far side is more about being seen.

• a shape for your lifestyle

If the goal is lap swimming for a little exercise, you'll need a rectangle so that you can move in a straight line and turn easily (pushing off a curve is not as easy as a flat surface). If you want something more organic, you can opt for an oval, a kidney shape, or an amorphous squiggle.

A small pool is perfect for dips, if that's all you intend to use it for. But if the goal is a place for kids to let off steam and horse around, you will want something with enough size that they can play some water games. Before choosing a shape, be sure that you can find a cover to fit it securely when not in use, for safety reasons. If you have a pool in a custom shape, you will need to have a cover specially made as well.

LEFT Even unusually shaped pools can be accommodated with pool covers. Here, you can see the automatic cover as it is closing. Many covers are made of heavy-duty vinyl, and can automatically remove rainwater that has collected on top.

LEFT This infinity-edge pool meanders in and out, creating a large space, much like a little pond. At the far end are misters that spray water to cool down sunbathers on the deck and add an element of fun.

SALTWATER POOLS

@ popular alternative to chemically chlorinating a pool is to turn it into a saltwater pool. This can be done to an existing pool as well as one that's being built. Proponents like it because it's a more natural approach to keeping the water clean. Plus, it doesn't dry out your skin, turn blonde hair green, or have the chemical odor that traditionally treated pools do.

The salt (which chemically speaking is simply sodium chloride) acts as the chlorinator when it is broken down into separate sodium and chloride molecules. The chloride acts in the same way that chemical chlorine does, but without all of the side effects.

Using saltwater also means you don't have to store as many chemicals poolside: only salt and your pH testing kit, which still are necessary, since if the pH is too high or too low the chloride is not as effective.

LEFT A round pool becomes the center of the backyard universe. Here, many elements rely on curves, circles, and half circles for their form. The brick coping carries through the concrete decking with lines that radiate in every direction. In the pool, the curved step is the perfect spot for in-water seating.

spas

● ● ● MANY OF US GO ON VACATION TO TAKE ADVANTAGE OF A SPA, so it's a true luxury to have in one's own backyard. But what exactly is a spa, and how does it differ from a hot tub? A hot tub is a freestanding prefabricated unit, while a spa is built into the ground and is often attached to the pool itself, allowing it to work off of the same filtration system. Spas and hot tubs essentially have the same therapeutic effect. And both can be winterized, so they can be used all year.

Today's spa is designed to relax and heal the body. Its temperature can be controlled easily, and should be around 100°F (104°F is the maximum number that is still safe, according to the Consumer Products Safety Commission; if you're pregnant or have a health problem, check with your doctor first).

LEFT A round spa, is completely separated from the pool by decking and coping.

BELOW An underwater bench in this spa offers a magnificent view of the pool.

LEFT A contemporary spa is separated from the pool by a decorative wall of glass tile.

FACING PAGE A stone spa spills into a larger pool for a naturalistic effect.

POOL SAFETY

As fun as pools are, they require vigilant monitoring, especially if you have small children in the house, or even in the neighborhood. Many municipalities have regulations requiring that pools be fenced-in on all sides (including between the house and the pool) using particular materials at specific heights. Even if you have no local regulations, the American Academy of Pediatrics advises the fence be at least 4 feet tall around the entire perimeter. Other tips: Install a fence that can be opened only if you enter from the house to prevent neighborhood kids from being able to act on their curiosity, and make it high enough that children can't reach the latch. Also opt for one that self locks.

The Association of Pool and Spa Professionals also suggests making sure that any suction outlet in the pool is properly covered with the appropriate device, and that the entire pool itself is covered, especially during the off season, with a material strong enough to withstand a person falling onto it. And just in case someone does fall in, always have a life ring and shepherd's hook nearby, so they can either float to the edge or be pulled to safety. Also be sure to store all of your pool chemicals in a locked cabinet or room.

LEFT Incorporating the elements of earth, fire, and water, this area is alive and inviting. The Japanese-soaking-tub-style spa on the left is easily accessible up the three steps.

From inside, this modern home has views to the spa and pool, thanks to the glass doors and walls. Everything outside relies heavily on straight lines and angles, which is in keeping with the style of the home.

• choosing
the right spa

How you design your spa depends on how you want to use it. If it's for therapy—to reduce stress or heal muscle injuries—you want to make sure the size can accommodate any exercises you may need to do. If it's for lounging with friends, make sure there's enough seating. Providing seating for at least four adults should suffice, unless you plan on large gatherings in the spa. And if you like the massage aspect, work with an expert to determine where to place the jets, to target muscles all over the body.

LEFT This teak deck cantilevers over the pool on one side. On the other side, a spa cover secured on a metal track can be slid over top with a gentle push of the foot.

TOP This circular spa is worked into the landscape with boulders and plantings for a naturalistic look. The curved wall of the pool merges with the outside curve of the spa.

BOTTOM In order to keep this large spa from taking over the space, the designer tucked one side of it into the hillside. She surrounded it with boulders to appear as if cushions to be sat upon.

•lap pools and swim spas

If you're a swimmer, a lap pool in the backyard puts exercise so close, there's no excuse. It is usually 25 meters long (the length of regulation pools) and is not very deep (usually 3 or 4 feet) because its sole purpose is for distance swimming. A lap pool tends to be narrow, the width of a single pool lane. If you have kids who like to play around in the pool, a lap pool might be too small for good rowdy fun.

If your yard doesn't have 25 meters to spare for an entire lap pool, you could opt for a "swim spa," which is a small pool with strong jets, against which you can swim in place. Not all pool builders can install a pool spa, so you may need to search to find the right installer.

A lap pool need not look like a dreary workout area. Here, the narrow pool is surrounded by box hedge and other greenery.

LEFT This lap pool almost points to the body of water in the distance like an arrow. The deck incorporates a diamond pattern that bookends the pool, giving it a fancy frame.

LEFT Located in the backyard of a riverfront property near Bangor, Maine, this pool is always warm enough for a swim (unlike the river). With chaises and other comfortable seating around it, the area is equipped for the lounger and the exerciser alike.

making shade

● ● ● GETTING INTO THE WATER CAN'T BE THE ONLY RESPITE FROM THE HOT SUN when you're poolside. Oases of shade can be achieved with a variety of approaches, and will cool you down even in the hottest weather. First, there's the umbrella, which with today's styles and fabrics is so much more attractive and user-friendly than it once was. You could also plant trees or shrubs to cast a shadow on the pool deck.

If the pool is near enough to the house, awnings extending from the exterior windows can provide some relief to sunbathers on the deck, as can freestanding structures like gazebos and pergolas made of cloth, wood, or even plant material.

Chaise lounges line up for some shade under this wood pergola. Elevating it two steps above the pool makes it feel like a destination, separate from the pool itself.

ABOVE
Tall cypresses and a variety of shrubs and other plantings create a perimeter of shade, without casting a shadow on the pool.

FACING PAGE TOP This covered porch sits practically on top of the pool, convenient for sunbathers who need to take a break. The vines hanging down the pillars create a nice composition visible from the pool.

FACING PAGE BOTTOM You don't need a pool house built of wood or brick to have the same effect. Here a weather-resistant cabana is assembled poolside for rest and relaxation.

Strawberry Mint Tea Sparkling Punch

by Fred Thompson

**Yields twenty 5-ounce punch-cup servings or
12 cocktail-size servings; about 3½ quarts**

2 pints fresh strawberries (about 1 pound),
   cleaned, hulled, and halve
2 tablespoons plus ½ cup granulated sugar
2 tablespoons fresh lemon-juice
⅛ teaspoon (or a good pinch) kosher salt
2¼ cups water
6 regular-size mint tea bags (not herbal tea),
   about ½ ounce total
6 cups cold water
1 liter (33.8 ounces) sparkling water, chilled
Mint sprigs for garnish (optional)
Whole fresh strawberries for garnish (optional)

❶ Put the strawberries, 2 tablespoons of the sugar, the lemon juice, and the salt in a food processor or blender. Process until it's a smooth purée, pour it into a container, and refrigerate until needed.

❷ In a small saucepan, bring 2¼ cups water to a gentle boil. Add the tea bags, remove from the heat, cover, and steep for 15 minutes.

❸ Pour the remaining ½ cup sugar into a 3-quart heatproof container (like a large Pyrex® liquid measure). Remove the tea bags when they're finished steeping (don't squeeze them) and pour the tea over the sugar, stirring to dissolve the sugar. Add 6 cups cold water and stir again. Chill until cold.

❹ To serve, combine the strawberry purée with the mint tea and stir well to mix completely.

If serving in a punch bowl, put the strawberry-mint tea in the punch bowl and slowly add the sparkling water. For individual servings, fill 10-ounce stemmed glasses (wineglasses work great) two-thirds of the way with the tea and top off with the sparkling water. Garnish with mint sprigs and a strawberry, if you like.

From *Fine Cooking* 52, p. 55

gallery

umbrellas

These days, an "umbrella" can mean so many things. Some are cantilevered, so they swing around to accommodate you as you adjust where you're sitting; some have the post attached to the side, rather than through the middle, so you can sit directly under it without having to navigate the pole. Others are wall mounted or can be placed in the pool itself, for shade while you swim. Some are made of aluminum, others of wood. Available shapes range from rectangular to octagonal to oval. Be sure the fabric offers UV protection. And if you live in an area prone to gusts, check to see if it's wind-resistant.

1 Pagoda-like tip.

2 Center pole round.

3 Doesn't obstruct views and can even be put into the pool.

4 Center pole square.

5 Cantilevered round with base of large tiles.

6 Razor-like contour rotates 360 degrees.

7 Cantilevered square.

8 Cantilevered round with base of small tiles.

3

4

7

8

the pool house

● ● ● THE POOL HOUSE IS ABOUT CONVENIENCE AND COMFORT, and should be closer or more accessible to the pool than the main house is. It can be a place to shower off and change after a swim, or a spot for a quick bite to eat, with a view of the pool, of the entire yard, or even of a vista beyond. Oftentimes the doors are perpetually open so that it functions as an extension of the pool deck, with shade and some seating that provide a respite from the hot sun.

A pool house also can function as an architectural anchor, a visual focal point unto itself. And it can offer additional indirect lighting for nighttime swims.

LEFT Sitting in the pool house offers a view of the pool and beyond to the Santa Monica mountains. If that's not enough to capture your attention, there is a TV on each side, and comfortable wicker furniture in which to relax. The terra-cotta roof tiles and roaring fire give it intangible charm and warmth.

RIGHT With a transition from full shade to full sun, this closed pool-house structure gives way to an open pergola and then onto an exposed pool deck. Everything, including the grill and pool, is centrally located so that no matter what the activity, everyone is together.

FACING PAGE Planning the pool area layout so that the pool is easy to access usually increases how much it is actually used. The French doors open onto a patio just a few steps from the pool.

Spiced Mixed Nuts

by Jennifer McLagan

Tossing the warm nuts in a warmed bowl helps the spiced butter coat the nuts evenly.

Yields 4 cups

1 pound (4 cups) mixed unsalted nuts
    (such as cashews, macadamias,
    walnuts, pecans, or almonds)
½ teaspoon ground coriander
½ teaspoon ground cumin
2 tablespoons unsalted butter
2 tablespoons dark brown sugar
2 tablespoons chopped fresh rosemary
¼ teaspoon cayenne
1½ teaspoons kosher salt

❶ Position a rack in the center of the oven and heat the oven to 350°F. Scatter the nuts on a rimmed baking sheet and bake, shaking the sheet a couple of times during baking, until the nuts are nicely toasted, 10 to 15 minutes.

❷ Meanwhile, set a small heavy skillet over medium-high heat. Sprinkle in the coriander and cumin and toast until aromatic, about 30 seconds. Remove the pan from the heat and add the butter, brown sugar, rosemary, and cayenne. Return the skillet to low heat and stir until the butter melts and the sugar dissolves, 2 to 2½ minutes. Keep warm.

❸ Tip the nuts into a large warmed bowl, pour the warm spiced butter over the nuts, and add the salt. Stir until the nuts are well coated. Taste for seasoning and add more salt if necessary. Let the nuts cool completely.

From *Fine Cooking* 75, p. 90c

FACING PAGE TOP The glass doors to this hexagonal poolhouse fold to the sides to reveal comfortable sofas in a living room. An outdoor shower lets swimmers rinse off before and after swimming.

FACING PAGE BOTTOM A shower room inside a pool house is set up to accommodate the whole gang. People tend to finish swimming around the same time, so having several showers with a wall of hooks and built-in benches makes it all less chaotic.

A pool house functions as a guest house for the stargazer. Minimally furnished with contemporary styles, the bedroom feels stylish yet welcoming. Even the fabric chairs are chic in their simplicity.

• comfort by the pool

You can stock the pool house with a variety of amenities to make hanging out by the pool supremely convenient. A small refrigerator, for instance, allows sunbathers to grab a refreshment to cool off if they're not in the mood to cool off with a dip. And of course a bathroom inside is a necessity if you'd like the pool goers to stay out of the main house, with their wet bathing suits and hair. This also holds true if you're entertaining by the pool: Your guests can use the pool house restroom instead of traipsing through the house.

•the function of a pool house

A pool house should always provide some storage, since any pool area requires lots of furniture, cushions, pool accessories, and cleaners that need to be kept somewhere, especially during the off-season. A pool house can also add seating options, especially when sunbathers want a respite from the blazing heat.

Some pool houses go beyond the basic functions and play several roles, doubling as an artist's studio or a guesthouse when extended family comes to town. Or it can simply be a place to retreat to watch TV or read a book, even when you're not actually using the pool.

LEFT An outdoor shower is incredibly refreshing, and one with doors and some privacy allows for a clean you can replicate only when you're out in nature.

FACING PAGE Placing an outdoor shower against the house makes it easy to install and affordable to tap into existing water lines. Here, a showerhead sits against the intricate stonework of a pool house and amid colorful blooms. At the base is a spigot that you can use to wash off just your feet if that's all you need.

pool enhancements

● ● ● SITTING POOLSIDE IS ABOUT MORE THAN JUST THE POOL; it's about the lighting, the décor, and all of the other little (and big) extras. If there's no comfortable and accessible seating, it's hard to enjoy a rest in the sun, so considering all of the extras is almost as important as the features of the pool itself.

Storage is paramount when there's so much pool "stuff," especially with children and all of the toys that make their summers fun. Water features also add interest to the area, as does the way you choose to light the area for after the sun sets.

ABOVE A light tucked under the canopy of an umbrella provides a nice soft glow for those gathered around.

RIGHT Setting the lights at the corners of each square of decking creates a pattern that mimics the twinkle of the stars. The grass growing around the lights adds to the texture with its shadows.

• lighting

Less can sometimes be more when it comes to lighting a pool. In fact, many people prefer to light the inside of the pool to create a romantic, relaxing nighttime atmosphere. Ideally, the lights in the pool will be placed so that you don't see the source but still get the overall glow. If the pool is close in proximity to the house, there can be residual light from outside porches or floodlights. Putting lights in a tree or shining a spotlight up into a tree can also provide softer, more subtle lighting.

For safety reasons, you will want to be sure to properly light the pool path, especially where there's a change in grade. But over illuminating the area can ruin the romantic vibe. Try fiber-optic lighting around or in the pool or to light up the edges of steps, plants, or even fountains. Fiber optics are illuminated with light, not electricity, so they don't get hot and are safe for water. Plus, they come in a variety of colors that can make hanging out by the pool a real show.

Different colors, shapes, and sizes of stone on this pool edge provide visual interest and texture, as do the differing heights of wall. The waterfall creates a lovely trickling so that even when you're not in the pool, you can listen to the soothing sound.

• decorative touches

The landscape surrounding the pool is crucial to the overall impression. For example, an elaborate flowering garden will draw the eye away from the water, even providing a focal point and beautiful view for sunbathers. To hide less appealing sights, such as the neighbor's house or a tool shed, you could use hedges or other greenery as a screen.

Naturalistic rocks encircling the pool can make it look almost like a topographical creation of Mother Nature. Mosaic tile along the top edge offers an artistic flair, almost like a fancy hat can make a beautiful face even more so.

LEFT What you put around the pool can really set the tone of the entire outdoor area. Here, the message is formal and traditional, with the equally spaced hedges and trees.

BELOW The choice of native plantings and the fact that the coping of the pool rests practically on top of the water makes this pool look like the edge of a pond or a lake.

BELOW Water spouts provide this pool with the melodic gurgle and splash of water hitting stones. The surrounding grasses add to the naturalistic vignettes that give the pool a finished look. The brick wall provides privacy and makes you feel like you're in a New Orleans courtyard.

RIGHT
Minimalist teak chaises have a low profile, in keeping with the contemporary home and pool.

TOP Bright red chaises make a statement at the edge of the water and offer a cozy poolside retreat.

RIGHT This pool's water level can be controlled so that islands of stone appear and disappear on a whim. Here, Adirondack chairs await visitors on one of those islands while the water is low.

• seating

The classic by-the-pool chair of choice is the chaise lounge. Some are on wheels, so they can be moved around the patio depending on where the sun is brightest. Some have reclining backs, so you can adjust for reading or for napping.

But there are lots of other options. A pool can be landscaped with smooth rocks or boulders along the edge that can be used as seating, or there can be grassy mounds for picnicking by the pool.

And there are in-pool seating options as well. An underwater ledge can be specially made for sunbathing, or steps can be designed deeper, so as to function as seating.

LEFT A romantic poolside swing for two is a great alternative when there are no cooling breezes. Vines scrambling up the pergola provide some shade and seclusion, and add to the atmosphere.

ABOVE In lieu of chaises, a bistro table and chairs make poolside dining easy. It's a great solution for casual meals, or even for morning coffee and reading the newspaper by the water.

• storage

Finding a place to keep all of those toys, tools, and towels can be a challenge, one that can be met with both permanent and portable solutions. For example, the pool house can be designed to offer ample storage.

If your property isn't big enough for an entire pool house, you could construct a small shed. Even more temporary are water-tight chests made of water-resistant materials or open baskets for toys. When planning out your new pool, be sure to keep storage in mind, without which you will be forced to lug all of those chair cushions and maintenance tools into and out of the house.

FACING PAGE
Pool houses needn't look like they're all about storage; they can be beautiful and functional. This California pool house covered in ivy matches the East Coast warmth of the Cape Cod–style main house, so it feels established and inviting.

LEFT A shed with sliding or pocket doors maximizes space and can hold bikes and other toys, as well as pool equipment.

BELOW LEFT
Tables and chairs that are lightweight can be easily stowed in a pool house at the end of the season, especially when it is this close. Cushions made of weather-resistant fabric can sit out in the rain, but they'll last longer if you take them in.

BELOW Part of this pool house is set aside for storing pool equipment, toys, and cushions. During the season, everything can be kept here, behind curtains; when it's too cold for swimming, it should be stowed in a cabinet or closet, where it's better protected from weather.

water features by the pool

● ● ● FEATURES IN THE POOL CAN ADD INTEREST, both visual and aural, by spraying, trickling, or spouting water into the pool itself. They can be hidden in plants that edge the rim, or they can trickle in via a waterfall, pipe, or ledge.

Your landscape designer can create one especially for you, or you can buy a prefabricated version that is relatively easy to install. They can spew water in the form of sheets, mist, or spouts. All give the pool a more organic feel, since water in nature is constantly moving and flowing as well.

ABOVE Spouts of water hidden amid plantings discreetly add the calming trickle of water. They can be installed along the edge of a swimming pool or reflecting pool for additional texture, color, and sound.

RIGHT Using wall art as part of a water feature makes the pool area feel almost like a furnished room. The contrast of the light-colored decorative medallion against the dark red of the brick makes it even more prominent.

LEFT Water cascades from a frosted-glass ledge onto this slide, which deposits kids directly into the pool. The whole setup is somewhat like a waterslide amusement park for the children, but also functions as a picturesque water feature for the grown-ups.

BELOW A reflecting pool is meant to mirror its surroundings. This one has motion sensors so that as someone passes, a series of water spouts activate, putting on a show as visitors approach the home.

LEFT A stacked Santa Barbara–stone fountain in the front yard can be dressed up with floating grasses or lotus.

ABOVE A runnel or rill of water meanders through the property and feeds into the pool. But who can resist playing in it along the way?

• nearby water features

The allure of a pool is its water. So it's no surprise then that many people want to carry that feature throughout their property with other water features. Fountains in all shapes and sizes add visual interest and attract the eye, a wonderful view from across the yard, even as you lounge by the pool.

They also provide a visual break from expansive flooring and plant materials and serve as an invitation to venture into a new space. Water features can also act as a link between a pool space and a garden space, tying together the materials and color palette, while incorporating new ones for added interest.

ABOVE Water runs over the top of a precast concrete bowl and down the sides of the ledger-stone base. Those two parts of this fountain rest in a basin that has a wide ledge where people can sit to take in the meditative sounds.

RIGHT A concrete water fountain in one corner of the yard draws the eye. The multicolored plantings that surround it encourage lingering, as the eye wants to inspect every bloom and every leaf. If the plantings were one color, it wouldn't have the same effect.

FACING PAGE BOTTOM A rustic fountain and fireplace complement each other by providing the beauty and sound of fire and water, two of the four basic elements.

garden rooms

5

• • •

NATURE LENDS A HELPING HAND WHEN YOU'RE DECORATING A GARDEN ROOM. Trees, shrubs, or other plantings make up one or more borders, establishing the space as a retreat. It is also perhaps one of the easiest rooms to decorate, since the walls, if there are any, are made of or covered in plant material that does the decorating for you.

Oftentimes a garden room is a hidden oasis, perhaps drawing people out to an area of the yard they otherwise wouldn't make use of. It becomes a destination. And it is best when you incorporate beauty through the colors you choose for plants and furniture, wonderful fragrances from the plant life, and soothing sounds from water features and wildlife.

The best thing about garden rooms is that you can create one almost anywhere. Even when you live in an urban setting, for example, you can turn a rooftop into a garden room and elicit the same effect. In the suburbs, you can use the garden room as a way to block out the view of your neighbor's home or dampen noise from the road when you're outside.

Garden rooms are so verdant and inviting, you can't help but be lured in. A peek down the path into this garden room creates intrigue and curiosity, and draws people in. Think about the composition of the space as you enter as much as when you're in it.

To create a garden room, select plants that will thrive in your area and with the conditions of your yard. Consider the sun exposure of your garden room, the other plant life in the area, and the maintenance required by any new plants. If you're not someone who loves to get out and work in the garden, you want to make choices that require little upkeep.

formal garden rooms

● ● ● THINK ABOUT A FORMAL GARDEN ROOM AND HEDGES USUALLY COME TO MIND. When a home has traditional architecture, it makes sense to carry that into the garden. The hedges themselves look tidy and sophisticated, but are also a helpful way to establish the boundaries of the garden room and even provide privacy.

Formal gardens tend to have angular and geometric shapes, and a sense of symmetry. And they often are parterres, with paths running amid the plantings, the boxwood topiary, and the fountains. The maze of the hedges can offer a visual pattern from inside as well, especially if your home is above the garden so that you can look down on it.

This garden room with pea gravel flooring was inspired by Japanese kare sansui, which are gardens of raked gravel and stone meant to represent streams, oceans, and mountains.

ABOVE Concrete pavers set at a 45 degree angle to the line of the house draw the eye to the garden, and make the space look smaller. This garden room is bordered by a low boxwood hedge and a few statuary.

LEFT Steps leading up to a garden room makes it even more of a destination. Once there, the view from this elevation provides a great view of the rest of the property. Pairs of tall cypress trees and a white wall and fountain lend an air of regality.

More about...
HEDGES

t echnically what makes a hedge a hedge is a row of trees or shrubs, but it has many functions. It acts as an architectural element, establishing one space from the other. It can also provide privacy, behave as a wind blocker, function as a backdrop to your other plantings, and even provide its own color with flowers or berries.

Knowing what you want out of your hedges is the best way to determine what to plant. If you live in a temperate climate but you want to see a green garden room year-round, choose evergreen hedges. Also find out about the foliage, flower, and berry colors so that you can plan the rest of your garden accordingly.

Consider maintenance as well. Formal angular hedges require more work than freeform hedges. And a plant with good disease resistance will fare best.

If privacy is a priority, opt for a dense, tall hedge for a complete screen, or one with a bit of laciness that lets in light but still provides seclusion. If bigger isn't better in your yard, consider using dwarf varieties. In general, evergreens are best for screening; deciduous shrubs establish a border, but won't block out as much.

Popular types of hedges include boxwood, privet, hawthorn, holly, and yew, but consider lilac or even blueberry bushes. A good strategy is to plant several different varieties, so that if disease or pests attack, the whole hedge won't be decimated. Consult with your local nursery for the options in your area.

informal garden rooms

●●● IF HEDGES AND PARTERRES AREN'T IN YOUR PLAN, you may opt for a more organic-style garden room: shrubs in lieu of boxwood hedges to create softer lines, and paths that wend around, rather than coming in at angles. Casual furniture can also set the mood for the garden, as can whimsical garden ornaments like sculpture, fountains, and even wind chimes.

Hardscape components, like stone flooring and walls, can add structure to any garden room, but they can be decidedly more casual in material and shape. A white picket fence, for example, sends a more informal message than one of wrought iron or stacked brick. And a berm used as a border is much more naturalistic, and less imposing, than a stone wall.

ABOVE It's fun to create an idyllic spot along a path where you can stop to take in the surrounding beauty. The circular gate opening allows visitors to see inside, which sends a friendly message that this gated garden is welcoming.

RIGHT An oasis in the middle of a neighborhood, this garden room features a horizontal slatted fence, which provides privacy but still lets in the light. The horizontal stripes created by the fence nicely harmonize with the graphic pattern in the concrete.

ECO-FRIENDLY STRATEGIES

When it comes to making a garden room environmentally green, there are several options. First, use "living" fences made of hedges. Birds like to eat the hedge's berries and seeds, and nest inside. Including a water source (fountain, pond, birdbath) is a sure way to attract wildlife, too, especially one with an alluring trickling noise. Also try to leave perennials into the fall so that birds can feed on the dried seeds.

Planting native varieties is also a way to be eco-minded. It minimizes maintenance, which in turn reduces the amount of water and energy you use. And indigenous creatures like indigenous plantings.

Finally, treat your garden without chemicals or pesticides, instead using natural pest control methods. Make it an organic habitat for the health of your family and your neighborly critters.

TOP With a variety of desert plants, this garden takes on an exotic air. The water in the fountain is percolated onto the gravel flooring, drained, and then recirculated.

ABOVE Adding comfy cushiony chairs and a coffee table to a garden room makes it even more appealing, and more like a home-outside-of-home.

LEFT The wrought-iron arbor covered in wisteria sinensis and white lady banks roses welcomes visitors into this dining area with a southern drawl.

dining in a garden room

●●● GARDEN ROOMS WILL ALMOST ALWAYS BE RELAXING. After all, the color green is renowned for its calming properties. But garden rooms can have a dual purpose. And very often that second purpose is as a place to eat. Green as the backdrop for a dinner really sets off the food and place settings.

Or you can implement a color theme. Perhaps your favorite color is purple, so you plant only varieties that will bloom in that color. You could also incorporate the common color into your décor, including purple dining chairs, pillows, and light fixtures.

LEFT
A pergola or trellis structure can be used to delineate a garden room and, because it's open at the top, still let in the sun. Sitting at this teak dining room table, you can take it all in.

FACING PAGE TOP The wide brick steps up to this secluded outdoor dining area welcome you with fanfare and let you know you have the best table in (or out of) the house.

FACING PAGE MIDDLE The destination here is clearly the dining table, as the path widens to encompass the circular shape of the "room." As you get closer to the table itself, the pavers are laid in formal pattern.

FACING PAGE BOTTOM The dining area on this patio is in the shade, thanks to an adjacent tree, but the clearing just beyond practically glows from the sunshine.

Balsamic Macerated Strawberries with Basil

by Sarah Breckenridge

To maintain a strawberry's beautiful shape, use a paring knife to remove the cap with an angled cut.

Yields 4 servings as a dessert; 6 to 8 as a filling or topping

2 pounds fresh strawberries, rinsed, hulled, and sliced ⅛ to ¼ inch thick (about 4 cups)
1 tablespoon granulated sugar
2 teaspoons balsamic vinegar
8 to 10 medium fresh basil leaves

❶ In a large bowl, gently toss the strawberries with the sugar and vinegar. Let sit at room temperature until the strawberries have released their juices but are not yet mushy, about 30 minutes. (Don't let the berries sit for more than 90 minutes.)

❷ Just before serving, stack the basil leaves on a cutting board and roll them vertically into a loose cigar shape. Using a sharp chef's knife, very thinly slice across the roll to make a fine chiffonade of basil.

❸ Portion the strawberries and their juices among 4 small bowls and scatter with the basil to garnish, or choose one of the serving suggestions below.

Serving Suggestions:

Serve the strawberries over grilled or toasted pound cake. Garnish with a dollop of crème fraîche.

Put the berries on split biscuits for shortcakes; top with whipped cream and scatter with the basil.

Layer the berries with ice cream or yogurt for a parfait. Garnish with the basil.

From *Fine Cooking* 86, back cover

garden gates

Putting a gate or entryway at the entrance to a garden room is a way to add intrigue. It creates a feeling of anticipation, and acts as an invitation to enter. The style of the gate should complement the style of the home: ornate metal, cottage-style white picket, naturalistic vine-covered trellis. You can also use the height of the gate to send different messages and set different tones: Low gates serve as a marker, distinguishing one area from another; tall gates are more restrictive.

1 Cottage garden gate with rose-covered arch.

2 Modern teak-framed frosted glass gate with stacked-stone posts.

3 Short slatted white gate with arch of roses.

4 Wrought-iron gate and fence with formidable concrete posts.

5 Blue wood-plank door, with ornate metalwork window and concrete walls.

1

garden room as a destination

●●● FINDING THE BEST SPOT FOR A GARDEN ROOM depends on your home and the layout of your yard. If you have enough acreage, you can create a garden room that is farther from the house than some of your other outdoor living areas. Unlike an outdoor kitchen or dining room, where you want the convenience of being able to go in and out of the house easily, a garden room can be an escape from the everyday and a place where you are physically and spiritually separated from the tedium of daily life.

The sights, sounds, and fragrances in a garden room will be completely dictated by nature, rather than what is coming from the house. No phone ringing, no visual reminders of the chores left undone; just the birds chirping and butterflies landing on nearby flowers, a complete respite.

TOP A path of Santa Barbara flagstone embedded in grass leads the way to a meditation garden surrounded by walls of privet. The fountain provides a soothing, mind-clearing trickle, while also appealing to birds who add to the tranquil symphony.

BOTTOM Sitting in one of these red cushioned chairs, your eye is drawn to the statue at the end of this long vista. The four tall cypress trees represent the four corners of the earth and lend an Italianate flavor, while also providing vertical punctuation to the composition.

FACING PAGE Stairs in the same flagstone pattern as the upper and lower patios practically pull you up and over to the tree, which acts as the anchor for the entire space. Using a variety of plantings and colors, rather than one monochromatic layout, encourages passersby to stop and take it all in.

a garden room near the house

● ● ● SOME OF THE LOVELIEST GARDEN ROOMS TAKE ADVANTAGE OF A HOME'S OUTSIDE WALL as part of the structure of the space. This is a great option if you have a courtyard or unused nook. It can still feel like just as much of a retreat when you strategically add some greenery, hardscape, and furnishings.

The style options are almost as wide open as if it were a separate, larger garden room. You can create a formal or casual space, neatly shaped or overflowing and organic. Just because your square footage is limited doesn't mean your options are.

FACING PAGE
Sitting in the lounge chairs and facing the lush garden, one forgets the house is at the back. Two container plantings with red blooms stand like sentries at the entrance to the path from the lawn. Making both the same color is a way to say "start here."

TOP Boxwood is the focus of this Louisiana home's back courtyard parterre. The ashlar pattern flagstone wraps around a center island of boxwood designs, taking you on a little journey. Urns and potted plants bring more color into the space.

BOTTOM This small courtyard feels spacious yet secluded. The walls of the home serve as the bones, but it's nicely filled in with container plantings and climbing vines.

More about...
DEALING WITH SHADE

🛈 f your garden room doesn't get much sun, you can still create a beautiful, lush space. Go for shade-loving plants, of which there is great variety. They tend to be deep green, with thick leaves. But there are flowering plants you can incorporate as well, like bleeding heart and vinca. The lighter the flower, the better it will stand out against the dark green of the foliage.

Use the colors of your plants to your advantage. For instance, to simulate the sun-dappled effect, choose variegated varieties, which have white or lighter green markings on the leaves. It will appear as if the sun is shining and reflecting off the leaves. Plants that are a lighter green—lime colored ferns, for example, which love shade—also fool the eye into thinking there's sunshine. Ferns, with their lacy fronds, add texture to a space too.

If your perennials don't add much color, turn to potted annuals that thrive in shade, like impatiens. They're a good way to bring in some color after spring blooms have come and gone.

container plantings

●●● CONTAINERS FILLED WITH ANY TYPE OF FOLIAGE AND FLOWER can add a lot to a garden room. First off, they provide a movable focal point, attracting the eye to any level or height you desire. If you have blooms only at the soil level, for instance, you can add some taller potted flowering plants for more visual interest and texture.

And the containers themselves become part of the structure and hardscape of the garden. Made of materials like terra cotta or stone, they provide a break from the monotonous greenery. The container plants can also be used to bring in more color, especially if you use annuals. And it's much easier to plant annuals in a pot than a planting bed that needs to be dug up frequently. In fact, container gardening is ideal for people who would like to minimize the time they spend maintaining the garden. It's also great if you have limited space.

FACING PAGE
Potted plants positioned at different heights create a layering of greenery in this lovely sitting area. The hard angle of the corner is softened by this collection of plants, which are housed in some unusual and whimsical containers that provide even more contrast and texture.

ABOVE A cluster of 36-inch-tall terra-cotta pots becomes a vegetable garden, with lettuces, herbs, and even tomato vines. Their height means you don't have to bend down to pick. Both practical and beautiful, the produce adds color to the garden and great flavor to the plate.

RIGHT A formal urn is softened with this shapely group of perennial succulents. It has taken about three years to get them this luxuriant. They are so low-maintenance, however, that they need to be watered only about every three months.

TOP Raised planting beds yield sun-kissed edibles all season long. The broad ledges around each bed provide a spot for a harvest basket, or to sit and take a rest. The cushioned benches at either end of this garden patch give the owners a spot from which to admire their handiwork.

BOTTOM In lieu of a railing, these rectangular terra-cotta planters delineate the edge of the stairs. When you reach the top, the payoff is another cluster of container plantings. This is especially appealing for urban dwellers, who often don't have access to a patch of ground for a garden.

FACING PAGE RIGHT This grouping of desert plants takes on a still-life quality, as if they're posing for a painter. The different sizes and shapes of the containers make for an interesting composition, as do the different sizes and shapes of the plants themselves.

RIGHT Poufs of lime-colored sweet potato vine and bursts of red begonias serve to soften the formality of this brick staircase and entrance. They also make the space more welcoming and lived-in.

•setting a mood with containers

Putting your plants in pots, urns, and other containers is another way to establish the style of your garden room. The material and shape of the container itself can elaborate on your garden's personality. You can use it to add lushness to a space, or to add splashes of color. It can be modernist and spare or full and regal; or it can provide a beautiful flourish, or be more practical, like vegetable plants that yield produce. They can be built into the ground, or be freestanding and movable with the season or the sun. They can even be hanging baskets to add colors and textures at eye level.

When you're planning out your garden room, take the container plantings into consideration from the start. Don't make them an afterthought.

garden lighting

●●● LIGHTING HAS A ROLE AS A PRACTICAL FEATURE AND AS A CREATOR OF AMBIENCE. Overdoing it, however, can ruin the mood you're going for and attract pesky bugs. Some of the best approaches are indirect. For example, hang lights in trees to imitate the light you'd get from a full moon, for a subtle, romantic effect (a technique aptly called moonlighting). Or you can place the lights on the ground and aim them to highlight trees, statues, or water features. This adds texture and establishes the features as destinations. Or plan your lighting so that it creates intricate shadows against a wall or floor.

Once you install basic lighting fixtures outside, you can accent with more temporary items, like outdoor lamps, tiki torches, and, everyone's favorite, votive candles. They add a personal, homey touch. Even if you don't plan to spend much time in the garden at night, lighting can make the view from indoors beautiful too.

Setting a spotlight at the base of a tree and directing it up will highlight the tree and bring out some interesting shadows. It can also serve to provide some perspective at night, when it's difficult to discern the distance to the water.

lighting details

Here is a glossary of garden lighting basics:

Low-voltage lighting. 12 volts, as opposed to 120 volts. Low voltage is popular for outdoors because you don't have to dig deep to install the wiring, it requires less energy, and it's safe when children, pets, and water are around. The 12-volt bulbs also tend to last longer and are available in a wider variety of colors and wattages.

Transformers. If you have a low-voltage lighting system, you need a transformer. They can handle anywhere from 100 to 1,000 volts, depending on what you need. When choosing how many volts you want, always give yourself a cushion in case you expand your garden (and your lighting) in the future.

Cables. They come in 8-, 10-, or 12-gauge thicknesses, and you need to make sure the one you get is appropriate for your lighting. The wrong size can cause the lighting to dim involuntarily.

Solar powered lights. These can be more expensive than regular low-voltage lights, but don't require any cords because they're completely powered by the sun. They usually need about 8 hours of sunlight during the day to work at night.

1 A vintage metal birdcage on a decorative metal base becomes a votive holder in the garden. It doesn't produce much light, but does provide a romantic ambient glow.

2 An innocent statue hiding amid the ferns with her basket of fruit doubles as a pedestal for a votive candle.

3 These weather-proof lamps have wickerlike shades and can withstand rain and snow. The "tree lamp" includes three smaller globes suspended from a floor lamp base.

4 Rustproof metal solar lights with sturdy bubble glass can line the edge of a garden, thanks to the ground stakes, or they can be removed to be used as table lanterns.

secluded spots

●●● IN THE YARD, FINDING THE PERFECT PLACE TO WHICH YOU WANT TO ESCAPE doesn't just happen. Careful planning is how you make your guest feel she has just stumbled upon a hidden gem. Think about how you approach the space (down a winding path or through a gate), how it is viewed from the house (if it's visible at all), and what the view will be once you're there. An entryway is one way to achieve this, as it almost whispers, "Please do come in, you've found the perfect spot!"

Sometimes this special place is great because it's in the shade. Or perhaps it's in the only sunny spot. If so, you will want to provide a shade option, like an umbrella or pergola, so that you always have a choice.

LEFT Sitting amid the dappled light of the tree canopy, these Adirondack chairs seem as if they have appeared out of nowhere. While the overall impression is one of forest-shaded beauty, the bricked path and planted annuals provide a more polished veneer.

FACING PAGE BOTTOM LEFT An archway covered in climbing vines sends the message as you approach that what lies on the other side is a secluded secret garden. The pagoda-like birdhouse adds to the childlike whimsy of discovering a special place that feels like your very own.

LEFT A hidden spot can even exist in plain sight. Turning a shaded corner of the patio or yard into a secluded spot makes it feel as if it's tucked away even when it's not. The planting beds practically envelop the chaises to give the impression of a hideaway, but with enough room at the foot to get in and out comfortably.

Clementine Granita

by Ruth Lively

This granita is a refreshingly light and delightful finish to a rich meal. And it's a snap to make. If you have an ice cream freezer, this recipe works equally well as a sorbet.

Yields 4 servings; about 1 quart

¾ cup granulated sugar
2 tablespoons finely chopped clementine zest
   (from 2 to 3 medium clementines)
Kosher salt
3 cups fresh clementine juice, with pulp
   (from 18 to 20 medium clementines or about 4 pounds)

❶ In a small saucepan, stir together the sugar, zest, a pinch of salt, and ¾ cup water. Bring to a boil over medium heat and cook, stirring, until the sugar dissolves and the syrup is clear, about 2 minutes. Set aside to cool slightly as you juice the clementines.

❷ Stir the juice and syrup together, pour into a small metal pan, such as a loaf pan, cover with plastic, and freeze for 2 hours. Stir the mixture with a spoon, breaking up the portions that have become solid, and return to the freezer. Stir every 30 minutes until the mixture is evenly icy and granular, about 2 hours more.

❸ Cover and return to the freezer until ready to serve. To serve, scrape with a spoon to loosen the mixture, and spoon into small bowls or glasses.

From *Fine Cooking* 82, p. 21

Allowing the plants to grow through the slats on this cushioned teak bench makes it look as if it is part of the landscape.

• more hidden gems

What a delight to find a seat or a table at the end of a path, when you thought there was nothing more. It's an ideal way to spend a lazy afternoon by yourself or with the company of a good book or a good friend. Foliage and flowers can provide camouflage and establish a sense of mystery.

Consider it your wonderful hideaway and adorn it with your favorite things, including comfy furnishings and fragrant flowers and plants. Choose a variety that bloom at different times throughout the year, so you always have the companionship of some flowers.

TOP Tall plantings create a dining area that feels screened from the rest of the yard and the neighbors. Hosting friends for an afternoon snack and glass of lemonade can feel more special than the effort you put into it—that's the magic of a secret garden.

BOTTOM Sturdy blue Adirondack chairs are enveloped by groundcover, so the seats appear as if an extension of the ground. The bamboo fence also adds to the seclusion. Having just a pair of seats creates the impression that it's reserved for a special couple.

• designing a path

A path is about more than just getting from one place to another. It's about the journey, which should be as beautiful, fragrant, and full of life as any other part of your garden.

How you approach creating the path depends on how you intend to use it, and who will use it. For example, making it narrow and curvy with bends will slow down traffic, which is a great tool if you have children who you don't want tearing through the area. Or perhaps you want a wide path so you can stroll with your loved one, side by side.

TOP A brick path leading up to a brick wall with a gate gives way to stone pavers and pea gravel as you step across the threshold. The change in material from mortared brick to loose stones encourages you to slow down to take in the surroundings.

FACING PAGE Linear paths keep the eye focused on the destination at the end. This path of brick laid in a running-bond pattern is framed by deep green grass, which creates such beautiful contrast, it resembles a carpet runner.

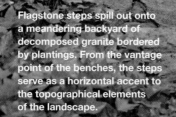

Flagstone steps spill out onto a meandering backyard of decomposed granite bordered by plantings. From the vantage point of the benches, the steps serve as a horizontal accent to the topographical elements of the landscape.

Stepping-stones in a grass lawn serve mostly as a guide for traffic. The recommended distance between them is 6 to 8 inches. The size of the stone or paver, however, depends on the size of the lawn. The scale should be such that an immense lawn doesn't dwarf its stepping stones or a small lawn isn't eaten up by them.

the shape of a path

When you look at your garden from afar, the path can serve as a design feature, creating a pattern. So instead of viewing a path as just a way to connect different parts of your yard, think of it as integral to the layout and design. That said, if the path isn't practical, it won't be used. It's important to find a balance between making it a pleasurable journey with bends and meanders and making it useful and efficient.

If you want two people to be able to walk side by side, make the path about 4 feet wide. For narrower single-file paths, you need about 2½ feet. The path should be made of a pervious material that allows water to seep through, or it needs to be sloped to facilitate proper draining. And if it's an oft-traveled path, put the pavers into a 2- to 3-inch cement base so that it won't need resetting as frequently.

TOP Sweetwater stones make up this path that merges from two into one. When joining two paths, the width at the point where they meet should be about two-thirds of what it would be were the paths side by side. And then it should gradually narrow back to the width of one.

BOTTOM Poured concrete slabs with pea gravel makes for a smooth path with a contemporary aesthetic. To prevent falling, the concrete and stones are kept at the same level. The pea gravel is refilled periodically, as rain and foot traffic can displace it over time.

• edging a pathway

What you choose to line the sides of your path with can totally change the experience of walking it. Using fragrant herbs and other plants along the edges means that when you brush by, you are inundated by a sweet, grassy, or herbal fragrance.

You can also use the path to hint at what lies ahead. If it leads to a hidden garden room, for example, use some of the same plants you put inside to tie them together. Plantings along the edges can also be used to give structure to a more freeform path, giving it a fixed shape and silhouette.

The light-colored concrete pavers and steps against the dark river rocks create a contemporary minimalism. It can be so striking that the pathway becomes a focal point as if a work of art.

ABOVE Plant growth between these concrete pavers serves to marry the path material with the plant material on either side by blurring the distinction and making one part of the other. Bright colors along the edge encourage walkers to look around and enjoy the surroundings.

ABOVE These steps were added in the 1980s to look original to this 1923 home. Full plantings along the edges serve to soften the concrete, which was given an aged patina by mixing in beer and yogurt, as well as dirt, campanula, and moss spores.

RIGHT Low-growing plants along the edge of a path help make the transition from path to landscape more gradual. The material of the path, decomposed granite, is best saved for areas farther away from the house, as its small granules can easily be tracked inside.

PATH MATERIALS

there are many options when it comes to what to use for a pathway, including decomposed granite, stone, wood, synthetic wood, mulch, concrete, sand, brick, and even turf. What you choose depends on what you want out of it, of course. Certain loose gravely materials, like pea gravel, will slow people down, for example, as they walk. If your site is sloped, gravel isn't ideal because it will roll off with a good rain or wind. Gravel is also best used far from the house, as it is frequently brought inside on shoes. But it's a popular choice because it's affordable and plentiful.

If you go with pavers, look for something that won't become slippery when wet. And if you live in a region with severe winters, choose a darker material so it will absorb heat from the sun and melt the snow and ice.

The materials used in the home and elsewhere in the yard should also play a role in determining your path. A common color or material, like brick, that appears throughout the home and yard ties all of the elements together, making it feel deliberate and cohesive.

LEFT A decomposed granite path is very low-maintenance. It serves the purpose of getting you from one spot to another, but it doesn't have to be purely utilitarian. Here, a purple-cushioned bench allows one to stop to appreciate the view.

FACING PAGE This path contains many materials: concrete slabs separated by an aggregate of river stones and pea gravel. The colors of the darker stones are mirrored in the stained dark square within the concrete; the lighter color of the concrete is echoed in the pea gravel.

RIGHT Baby tears, a shade-loving groundcover, grows between irregularly shaped Arizona rosa flagstone, whose terra-cotta coloring relates to the terra-cotta tile roof on the house.

garden structures and ornaments

●●● GARDEN ROOMS BECOME SO MUCH MORE INTERESTING and practical when they are created with more than just foliage and flowers. Social, functional, and whimsical structures and ornaments can provide a solid architectural feature that anchors the garden. And they can add useful space for all kinds of activities and tasks.

A garden gathering is so much more of an event if you have a designated place in which to mingle, eat, and kick back. This can be achieved with any manner of structure, both permanent and modular. It can be a place to lounge around or dine in, and is often a retreat from the sun with some sort of provision for shade. Keep in mind as you arrange the furniture and determine the layout that it's ideal to have a view of the surroundings for everyone, no matter which seat they choose.

ABOVE Reminiscent of a tree house, this structure has two levels of entertaining space. The stone pillars at the base tie in with the stone wall, but also maintain the naturalistic air of the wood deck up top, where there is a porch swing to take in the view—a favorite with the kids.

RIGHT An umbrella with gossamer fabric extensions turns a dining table and patio into a bona fide room. The fabric is loose enough to let breezes through but tight enough to keep bugs out. The overall impact: To dine here is to receive the royal treatment.

LIGHTING THE PATH

because pathways often contain uneven pavers or steps, seeing at night is imperative. Look for lights that shine downward, like bollard or tier lights. Most path lights shine with a radius of 6 feet, so putting them 12 feet apart would be enough to illuminate everything without overlapping.

Even if they're there, lights don't have to be visible. They could be nestled between boulders that line the path, so the light emanates from the edging, doing the job without the fixture staring at you.

ABOVE
Solar-powered slate stepping-stones with LED light.

MIDDLE LEFT
Copper path lights that weather well.

MIDDLE RIGHT
An arbor lit with low-voltage lights marks the start of the path to a fountain.

BELOW Bathing a wall in light to illuminate a path and highlight grasses.

ABOVE
An outdoor sink with ample counter space is ideal for avid gardeners. Locating it near or up against the house makes tapping into water lines easier and less expensive. A shelf over top is a great place to stash your collection of pots.

RIGHT A potting shed that's beautiful inside and out. The homeowner needed a larger shed than the one that had been there, so she carefully pulled off the vines that had grown around it, placed them in a tree, and re-adhered them to the new structure, giving it the appearance of longevity. From inside, the views are framed by the arches, so she can take in the scenery while at work.

FACING PAGE Expansive windows on an office or guesthouse brighten up the interior with plenty of sunlight. Curtains that extend just more than halfway up the doors provide enough privacy, but still allow the light to flood the space.

• functional garden structures

A shed or other utilitarian garden necessity doesn't have to be an eyesore. In fact, it can be a fundamental part of the garden landscape. It can act as a focal point, or it can blend in so well that it's hardly noticed. Its placement amid the plantings also means that when you're inside, you are rewarded with magnificent views of all of your hard work, so keep that in mind as you plan for windows and doors. Entertaining in the garden is so much more of a pleasure when you don't have to apologize for your shed's state of disarray.

ABOVE A whimsical rooster statuary and a sweet metal bird figure attached to a wall, which is covered in moss and tiny sedums, reside in a garden as a reminder to the homeowner to think of the birds as she's working in and planning her garden. She strives to provide places for them to roost and dine.

• whimsical garden ornaments

When placed throughout a garden, sculptures, fountains, and other artful pieces can inject a little personality in the most surprising ways. You can use them to add a bit of whimsy, or as a nod to a certain art form or era that you adore. When your garden isn't in bloom and appears almost exclusively green, a bright piece of art can bring in some much needed color. And something like a stone fountain can provide a visual break in all of the greenery and tie in nicely with the flooring and pathway materials.

TOP An African-American tradition in the South, the bottle tree is said to capture evil spirits, which, when the wind blows, legend has it, you can hear trapped inside. Many bottle trees are made using found bottles of all colors, but this one has a monochromatic cobalt collection that stands out well against the light wall.

LEFT The Greek goddess of youth, Hebe is the cup-bearer for the gods. Here, she is performing her duty as she offers up wine. The blooms of wisteria that hang in clusters are reminiscent of grapes and tie into the mythology as well.

LEFT A whimsical, fun expression of a chair, this piece of art is constructed from the chrome on a car. Because chrome can become scalding hot in the sun, the slats are made of a less heat-absorbing material.

BELOW The vast expanse of green seen here is broken up by unusual stone chairs and a table made to look like cushiony living room furniture: an armchair, a side chair, and a coffee table.

A chair transformed into a planter becomes a living piece of art. It loses its function as a place to sit down, but the white legs and back become a frame for a mixture of colorful annuals.

FURNITURE AS ART

Sure, a seat should be comfortable. But it can also be beautiful, enough so that it's a piece of art in your garden. The breadth of your creativity is the only limitation when it comes to how furniture can function as art. And you can make it have a dual purpose: for seating and for visual pleasure—the perfect marriage of form and function.

Creating a seat or sofa that is covered in sod, for example, is a great way to add whimsy to a garden room while also providing a spot to kick back. Build the frame of a sofa out of chicken wire, cover it with sod, and you have an adorably comfortable grass couch.

resources

PRODUCT SOURCES

Big Green Egg®
770-938-9394
www.biggreenegg.com
(grills and smokers)

Caspariˢᴹ
800-227-7274
www.casparionline.com
(luxury paper goods)

Fire Stone®
Home Products
866-303-4028
www.firestonehp.com

Frontgateˢᴹ
888-263-9850
www.frontgate.com
(outdoor living and home furnishings)

Fuego®
888-88-FUEGO
www.fuegoliving.com
(grills)

Gaiam®
877-989-6321
www.gaiam.com
(outdoor living and home furnishings)

Grandin Roadˢᴹ
866-668-5962
www.grandinroad.com
(outdoor living and home furnishings)

Kalamazoo
Outdoor Gourmet®
800-868-1699
www.kalamazoogourmet.com
(grills and outdoor appliances)

Lux Entertainment
866-684-3036
www.luxoutdoor.com
(outdoor entertainment and TVs)

Outdoor Lighting
Perspectivesˢᴹ
877-898-8808
www.outdoorlights.com
(garden, pool, and landscape lighting)

Smith & Hawken®
800-940-1170
www.smithandhawken.com
(patio and garden furnishings)

Sport Court Internationalˢᴹ
800-421-8112
www.sportcourt.com
(backyard game courts)

Sunbrella
336-221-2211
www.sunbrella.com
(weather- and sun-resistant fabrics)

Treasure Garden, Inc.®
www.treasuregarden.com
(outdoor umbrellas)

Tuuci®
305-634-5116
www.tuuci.com
(outdoor umbrellas)

Valeur
www.valeur.nl
(modern outdoor furnishings)

Vermont Castings®
800-668-5323
www.vermontcastings.com
(grills, fireplaces, hearths, and stoves)

Viking Range Corporation®
888-VIKING1
www.vikingrange.com
(grills and other outdoor appliances)

DESIGNERS

Angie Coyier Landscape Architecture
Santa Monica, CA
310-266-1941
www.coyierdesigngroup.com
angie@coyierdesigngroup.com

ARTECHO Architecture and Landscape Architecture/Pamela Palmer
Venice, CA
310-399-4794
310-399-3294
www.artecho.com

Heather Lenkin of Lenkin Design
Pasadena, CA
626-441-6655
www.lenkindesign.com
heather@lenkindesign.com

Katie Moss Landscape Design
katiemoss.com
katie@katiemoss.com
310-569-5333

Tineke Triggs with Artistic Designs for Living
San Francisco, CA
415-567-0602 office
415-606-8666 cell
www.artisticdesignsforliving.com
tineke@sbcglobal.net

Wendy Harper & Associates Landscape Architecture
805-529-3074
www.wendyharper.com
wendylharper@aol.com

MAGAZINES & WEBSITES

Casual Living
www.casualliving.com

Fine Cooking
www.finecooking.com

ORGANIZATIONS

The American Institute of Architects
202-626-7300
www.aia.org

Association of Pool and Spa Professionals
703-838-0083
www.apsp.org

Association of Professional Landscape Designers
717-238-9780
www.apld.org

American Society of Landscape Architects
202-898-2444
www.asla.org

Hearth, Patio & Barbecue Association
703-522-0086
www.hpba.org

National Association of Home Builders
800-368-5242
www.nahb.org

National Spa & Pool Institute
703-838-0083
www.nspi.org

photo credits

pp. ii–iii: Photos © Mark Lohman Photography

p. vi: (photo 1) Photo © Mark Lohman Photography, Design: Heather Lenkin of Lenkin Design; (photo 2) Photo courtesy Smith & Hawken; (photo 3) Photo © Mark Lohman Photography, Design: Grisamore Design; (photo 4) Photo © Jack Coyier Photography, Design: Wendy Harper & Associates Landscape Architecture; (photo 5) Photo © Jack Coyier Photography, Design: EPT Design

p. 1: Photo © Andrew Drake, Design; Kris Sargent

p. 2: (left) Photo © Jack Coyier Photography, Design: Wendy Harper & Associates Landscape Architecture; (right) Photo © Chipper Hatter, Design: Jeffrey Carbo ASLA

p. 3: Photo © Deanie Nyman Photography, Design: Patricia Benner Landscape Design

CHAPTER 1

p. 4: Photo © Bob Greenspan (www.bobgreenspan.com), Design: Alan Mascord Associates

p. 5: (top) Photo © Mark Lohman Photography; (top middle) Photo courtesy Viking Range, Corp.; (bottom middle) Photo © Mark Lohman Photography, Design: Heather Lenkin of Lenkin Design; (bottom) Photo © Jack Coyier Photography, Design: Katie Moss Landscape Design

p. 6: Photo © Olson Photographic LLC, Design: Peter Cadoux Architects

p. 7: (top & bottom) Photos © Jack Coyier Photography, Design: Ania Lejman Design Company

p. 8: Photo courtesy Fire Stone Home Products

p. 9: (top) Photo © Jack Coyier Photography, Design: Katie Moss Landscape Design; (bottom) © Mark Lohman Photography

p. 10: Photo © Chipper Hatter

p. 11: (top) Photo © Olson Photographic LLC, Design: Benchmark Builders; (bottom) Photo © Jessie Walker Associates

p. 12: (top) Photo © Chipper Hatter, Design: Kevin Harris Architect; (bottom) © Jack Coyier Photography, Design: Wendy Harper & Associates Landscape Architecture

p. 13: Photo © Olson Photographic LLC, Design: Pembrooke/Caledon, John Klein

p. 14: (top) Photo © Mark Lohman Photography, Design: Heather Lenkin of Lenkin Design; (bottom) Photo © Jack Coyier Photography, Design: Katie Moss Landscape Design

p. 15: (top) Photo © Ken Gutmaker Photography, Design: Rehkamp Larson Architects, Inc.; (bottom) Photo © Mark Lohman Photography

pp. 16–17: Photos © Jack Coyier Photography, Design: Katie Moss Landscape Design

p. 18: Photo © Jessie Walker Associates, Design: Doug Wierenga Builder

p. 19: Photo © Chipper Hatter, Design: Eduardo J. Jenkins Landscape Architect and Planner

p. 20: Photo © Mark Lohman Photography, Design: Heather Lenkin of Lenkin Design

p. 21: (top left) Photo © Jack Coyier Photography, Design: Katie Moss Landscape Design; (top right) Photo © Jack Coyier Photography, Design: Angie Coyier Landscape Architect; (bottom left) Photo © Mark Lohman Photography, Design: Heather Lenkin of Lenkin Design (bottom right) Photo © Jack Coyier Photography, Design: Wendy Harper & Associates Landscape Architecture

p. 22: Photo courtesy Viking Range Corp.

p. 23: (top left) Photo courtesy Smith & Hawken; (bottom left) Photo courtesy Kalamazoo Outdoor Gourmet; (right) Photo by Scott Phillips, courtesy *Fine Cooking* © The Taunton Press, Inc.

p. 24: (left & center right) Photos courtesy Kalamazoo Outdoor Gourmet; (top right) Photo courtesy Viking Range Corp.; (bottom right) Photo courtesy Fuego North America

p. 25: (left) Photo courtesy Kalamazoo Outdoor Gourmet; (right) Photo courtesy The Big Green Egg

p. 26: Photo © Jack Coyier Photography, Design: Wendy Harper & Associates Landscape Architecture

p. 27: (photos 1, 2, 3, 6): Photos courtesy Kalamazoo Outdoor Gourmet; (photo 4) Photo © Tria Giovan Photography; (photos 5, 7): Photos © Jack Coyier Photography, Design: Wendy Harper & Associates Landscape Architecture; (photo 8): Photo © Jack Coyier Photography, Design: Angie Coyier Landscape Architect

p. 28: Photo © Jack Coyier Photography

p. 29: (top) Photo © Jack Coyier Photography, Design: Angie Coyier Landscape Architecture; (bottom left) Photo © Jack Coyier Photography; (bottom right) Photo © Mark Lohman Photography, Design: Heather Lenkin of Lenkin Design

p. 30: Photo © Jack Coyier Photography, Design: Wendy Harper & Associates Landscape Architecture

p. 31: (top left & right) Photos © Jack Coyier Photography, Design: Katie Moss Landscape Design; (bottom) Photo © Mark Lohman Photography, Design: Heather Lenkin of Lenkin Design

CHAPTER 2

p. 32: Photo © Ken Gutmaker Photography, Design: Tineke Triggs with Artistic Designs for Living

p. 33: (top) Photo © Andrew Draken, Design: Kris Sargent; (top middle) Photo © Mark Lohman Photography; (bottom middle) Photo © Chipper Hatter Photography, Design: Jeffrey Carbo ASLA; (bottom) Photo © Jack Coyier Photography, Design: Angie Coyier Landscape Architecture

p. 34: Photo © Chipper Hatter Photography, Design: Jeffrey Carbo ASLA

p. 35: (top) Photo © Mark Lohman Photography, Design: Deborah Rhein; (bottom) Photo © Mark Lohman Photography, Design: Barclay Butera, Inc.

p. 36: Photo © Mark Lohman Photography

p. 37: (top left) Photo © Olson Photographic LLC, Design: Richard Swann Architect, Fairfield, CT; (bottom left) Photo © Mark Lohman Photography; (right) Jessie Walker Associates

p. 38: Photo © Jack Coyier Photography, Design: ARTECHO Architecture and Landscape Architecture/Pamela Palmer

p. 39: (left) Photo © Jack Coyier Photography, Design: Katie Moss Landscape Design; (top right) Photo © Tim Street-Porter; (bottom right) Photo © Ken Gutmaker Photography, Design: Tineke Triggs with Artistic Designs for Living

p. 40: Photo © Tria Giovan Photography

p. 41: (top left) Photo © Andrew Drake, Design: Kris Sargent; (bottom left) Photo © Andrew Drake, Design: Charlotte Behnke & John DeForest; (right) Photo © Ken Gutmaker Photography, Design: Tineke Triggs with Artistic Designs for Living

p. 42: Photo © Mark Lohman Photography, Design: Design Line Interiors

p. 43: (top left) Photo © Tim Street-Porter, Design: Nancy Goslee Power; (top right) Photo © Tria Giovan Photography, Design: Michael Goldberg; (bottom right) Photo by Scott Phillips, courtesy *Fine Cooking* © The Taunton Press, Inc.

p. 44: Photo © Jack Coyier Photography

p. 45: (top) Photo © Jack Coyier Photography; (bottom left) Photo © Tria Giovan Photography, Design: Suzanne Rheinstein; (bottom right) Photo by Scott Phillips, courtesy *Fine Cooking* © The Taunton Press, Inc.

p. 46: Photo © Mark Lohman Photography, Design: Heather Lenkin of Lenkin Design

p. 47: (left) Photo © Jessie Walker Associates, Design: Pilar Simon; (right) Photo © Jack Coyier Photography

p. 48: Photo © Chipper Hatter

p. 49: (left) Photo © Scot Zimmerman Photography, Design: Inn of the 5 Graces; (top right) Photo courtesy Fire Stone Home Products; (bottom right) Photo © Jack Coyier Photography

p. 50: Photo courtesy Fire Stone Home Products

p. 51: (top left) Photo © Tim Street-Porter, Design: Jeff Andrews; (bottom left) Photo © Jack Coyier Photography, Design: Katie Moss Landscape Design; (right) Photo © Chipper Hatter

p. 52: (top) Photo © Jack Coyier Photography; (bottom) Photo © Chipper Hatter, Design: Kevin Harris Architect

p. 53: (left) Photo © Tria Giovan Photography; (right) Photo © Jack Coyier Photography

p. 54: (left) Photo © Mark Lohman Photography; (right) Photo courtesy Smith & Hawken

p. 55: Photo © Mark Lohman Photography, Design: Heather Lenkin of Lenkin Design

p. 56: (photo 1) Photo © Tria Giovan Photography; (photos 2, 3, 4) Photos © Jack Coyier Photography; (photos 5, 6) Photos courtesy Smith & Hawken

p. 57: Photo © Jack Coyier Photography

p. 58: (top right & left) Photos © Jack Coyier Photography; (bottom) Photo © Mark Lohman Photography, Design: Heather Lenkin of Lenkin Design

p. 59: (top left & bottom right) Photos © Jack Coyier Photography; (top right) Photo courtesy Grandin Road; (bottom left) Photo © Tria Giovan Photography, Design: Suzanne Rheinstein

p. 60: Photo © Ken Gutmaker Photography, Design: Tineke Triggs with Artistic Designs for Living

p. 61: (photo 1): Photo © Tria Giovan Photography, Design: Trip Hoffman; (photo 2) Photo © Jessie Walker Associates; (photo 3): Photo © Mark Lohman Photography, Design: Heather Lenkin of Lenkin Design; (photo 4): Photo © Jack Coyier Photography, Design: Angie Coyier Landscape Architect; (photo 5): Photo courtesy Fire Stone Home Products

CHAPTER 3

p. 62: Photo © Mark Lohman Photography, Design: Harte Brownlee & Assoc.

p. 63: (top) Photo courtesy Frontgate; (top middle) Photo © Tim Street-Porter, Design: David Hertz; (bottom middle) Photo © Tim Street-Porter; Design: Brad Dunning; (bottom) Photo © Chipper Hatter

p. 64: Photo © Chipper Hatter